MW00585426

Barbie:

The Icon, The Image, The Ideal

An Analytical Interpretation of the Barbie Doll in Popular Culture

Kristin Noelle Weissman

Universal Publishers/UPUBLISH.COM
1999

Copyright (c) 1999 Kristin Noelle Weissman
All rights reserved.

Published by Universal Publishers/uPUBLISH.com
USA - 1999

ISBN: 1-58112-828-2

www.upublish.com/books/weissman.htm

Acknowledgments

I would first like to thank Dr. Shekhar Deshpande for his continual dedication, insight and inspiration throughout this endeavor, and during my four years of study at Beaver College. I would also like to thank Dr. Lisa Holderman and Dr. Annette Halpin for their time and genuine guidance while writing this thesis.

To my fellow students of communications at Beaver College: thank you for each of your unique contributions to the completion of this project.

To my fellow colleagues: thank you for your thorough knowledge into the study of the Barbie doll, without which this text would not be possible.

Above all, thank you to my Mom, Pat Weissman, my Dad Bill Weissman, family, and friends who gave me their special love and support which truly made this work complete.

Table of Contents

Chapter Four: Discussion
Part Two: Marketing Analysis

Chapter Five: Conclusion

Chapter Six: Bibliography

Chapter One
Introduction

Statement of Objectives

This thesis is a cultural analysis of: a) women's idealized perception of the Barbie doll, and b) the construction of the Barbie doll image through marketing. In addition, both areas will provide a concentrated emphasis on "respectability." The analysis will be focused on Barbie's creation in 1959, and on the current practices of representations in 1999.

The thesis is divided into two phases. Phase one illustrates the interpretation of how women perceive Barbie, and how they see themselves in her likeness. It further explores the determined impression of the doll as "respectable." Phase two examines the way that Barbie is presented in the market and the techniques used to formulate the intended representations of the doll. The analysis of the thesis focuses solely on her introduction in 1959, and on her current distinction.

The Barbie doll is an iconic image. The symbol of the "feminine ideal" which has caused women to perceive and recognize this figure in a personal light. Further, her existence in the marketplace creates a continual awareness in women to identify and evolve with this object as she captures the culture.

It is critical to examine the conception and portrayal of an icon such as the Barbie doll. As a predominant feature in American culture and society, she is a fictitious character that many have contrived into a reality. She is a name that strikes instant familiarity, and she is a name that evokes controversy, emulation, and success. This thesis achieves a comprehensive look into her importance to women, and the ways in which her corporate creators make her accessible to fulfill this need. Therefore, this thesis accurately makes a connection between the marketing of the Barbie doll, and the building of an icon.

Background

"Barbie You're Beautiful" is the 1959 theme song that introduced this 11 ½ inch doll into our lives 4 decades ago. It is also an accurate description of the distinctive product ascendancy and the reasoning behind the symbolic impact on women. For many years, the continued phenomenon of the Barbie doll has sparked unequivocal contention, and has led to the development of an idealized icon that women have challenged or accepted.

"She is a universally recognized image, but what she represents to women everywhere can be as personal as a fingerprint" (Lord 1). The construction and creation of the Barbie doll in 1959 marks not only the beginning of a thriving product, but the start of a model image that women have continually viewed as superior, unrealistic, or quintessential.

The presence of Barbie is pervasive throughout American society. She has taken on the appearances and vocations of many, and has therefore attempted to become an ideal. The attention and scrutiny that this doll has received, whether positive or negative, demonstrates to be exceptional. The resounding efforts of communications practitioners both in business and in the media, as well as in cultural studies, have established a world-wide recognition, debate, and adoration of the Barbie doll. She has acquired a human-like identity within our culture, and has spawned a historical sensation whose ability to captivate is timeless.

The address read 6058 South Western Street in Los Angeles, CA. This was the location where Ruth and Elliot Handler, and intimate colleague, Matt Matson, joined in 1945 to begin their own establishment. They proclaimed that with Elliot's designs, Matt's fabrication skills, and Ruth's marketing expertise, they had all of the central elements of a promising venture. By combining "Matt" and "El," they became Mattel, a contemporary, billion-dollar corporation. However, they were unaware that the individual left out of the naming of the profitable firm, would be the mastermind behind their most valuable product (Cook 1).

Ruth Handler devised and created the prototypal Barbie doll. After watching her daughter Barbara, from whom Barbie received her name, and her small friends behold ceaseless enjoyment from paper dolls, an idea occurred to Handler: "Why not mass produce a three-dimensional, sharply dressed version of these paper commodities?" Shortly after, on a trip to Germany, she came into contact with "Lili." She reigned as the star of an existing German cartoon, who was constructed into an 11 ½ inch beauty, designed for the primary pleasure of men as a "comical gift" (Groves 8).

By this time in 1958, Mattel had become a leading maker of action toys for young males, and Ruth saw the concept of Lili as an infallible way to even the market and collect a greater share for the enterprise. The rights to Lili were soon purchased, and the blonde bombshell was turned into the original brunette Barbie. Immediately, Mattel marketed her as the super model who had everything that little girls should crave: fame, wealth, and attention. "Successful gimmick, obviously" (Schneider 2).

Today, 39 years later, Handler says that "Barbie is an institution, and has been copyrighted as a work of art." In addition, critical author M.G. Lord has stated that "Barbie is a direct reflection of the cultural impulses that formed us. Barbie is our reality. And unsettling though the concept may be, I don't think it's hyperbolic to say: Barbie is us." Therefore, in order to accurately assess the presence of Barbie in the market and in our minds, this analysis is properly divided into two major classifications: cultural and corporate. The organization of the thesis is comprised of the following elements.

The analytical perspective, focused on in the discussion, examines how and why women cast themselves into the image of Barbie. This includes why they feel the compulsion to identify with this doll, and how she is conceived within our culture. In addition, this idea is expanded further to discover her representation, and define the semblance of Barbie culturally and perceptively through the eyes of women. This features the means that women exclusively embrace to position themselves into the image of Barbie. This is a significant portion of the analytical section. However, a specific look into the life of Cindy

Jackson, a woman who has modeled herself into a living Barbie doll, is also examined (Berens 1).

Why would anyone want to completely reconfigure their face and body, and risk their life to many complicated and dangerous surgical procedures just to look like *someone* else? Jackson not only aspires to do this, but she resolves to look like *something* else— a Barbie doll. To her, this is the ultimate woman, and to look like her is the ultimate power. Therefore, she is on a quest for domination and control over men and over society. She says that "life rewards you for who you are, not what you are." If her look ever fades, she discerns that she will be forced to abandon this world. The one where only the Barbie mask is acceptable. This is her perception of beauty and achievement in the current culture, and she does not endure alone. Since her reformation, Jackson has inspired a recognizable "army of clones" (Harris 2).

Following this segment, the marketing analysis begins by discussing the development of Barbie through the Mattel corporation in 1959. It also examines her statistics as a business toy product. This includes her profits, product position, and consumer demand.

Barbie remains "immune to the ravages of time" which is one reason for her powerful command (Chamberlain 59). Mattel has made sure that she can consistently adapt to the culture, and to the target audience. The product is flexible enough to accept the transition within society, and correlate all consumer needs. In addition, corporate facts such as her creation as a $2 billion industry, the realization that there are more Barbies in existence than people, and that close to every young female owns approximately eight of these dolls, greatly contributes to this business revolution (Mattel 1). Each of these issues are further addressed in the discussion.

The discussion begins to look more closely at the production aspects of Barbie and prove her marketable strengths. It analyzes where she falls in the market today and how she establishes her prominence. It also includes the manufacturing of not only a wide variety of dolls, but the popular culture that Mattel has created with this icon.

Other areas explored throughout this theme are her reliability in the toy world, the creation of her "classic image," and the brand loyalty that she has gained from consumers everywhere viewing her as the "All American Doll." Also, it is important to mention the way that Mattel has designed her instant recognition through packaging, style, and marketing mix. Even the color pink, that has prevailed unaltered throughout the years, serves as an identifiable factor which accompanies her consistently in some way (McKenzie 1).

The expanse of Mattel's reach is ardent and vast. There is a variety of Barbie dolls that converge consumer tastes and needs from children to collectors. The final point that is illustrated in this selection is the new Barbie currently in the design stage. For 40 years, this doll has remained physically the same with different accessories, and for the first time, a more lifelike dimensional Barbie will be introduced (McKenzie 1).

This is a precarious approach for Mattel because although they are implementing the assertion that they are more socially aware, they are also tempting the idea that if something works, why change it?

Finally, this thesis connects both the business and analytical perspectives. The examination of the longevity of Barbie in the market place is united to the ways in which Mattel has facilitated women's identification with this doll. Also, it incorporates how Mattel focuses on this desire within women, and apprehends their interest through marketing. Therefore, does the image of "Barbie You're Beautiful" simply say it all? To study the Barbie doll, one must have the ability to hold seemingly contradictory idea's in one's head at the same time— which, as F. Scott Fitzgerald has said is "the test of first rate intelligence" (Lord 2).

Outline

The outline of the thesis has been presented and interpreted in the "Background" section stated above. However, a brief description of later chapters is provided for clarification and understanding.

Chapter Two is comprised of the **Literature Review**. This chapter extensively examines the previously written works in the field, and states their contribution and relevance to the topic.

Chapter Three is the **Methodology** of the thesis. This describes how the thesis was performed, and what approaches and techniques were maintained.

Chapter Four provides the **Discussion and**

Analysis. This chapter shows what was discovered throughout the thesis.

Chapter Five addresses the **Conclusions.** This determines the final outcome of the analysis.

Chapter Six presents the **Bibliography**. It is a collection of both primary and secondary sources which have contributed to the extensive knowledge of this thesis.

Chapter Two
Literature Review

The mass media— As a primary and effective communicator to society, it depicts the representations of ideal images for women and for men. The mass media establishes ideological standards that if achieved, will equate with happiness and acceptance. Currently, the construction of gender as a paradigm of visual imagery, continues to dominate the scope of media representations. Therefore, the media could be characterized as being aggressively motivated by the conceptualization of gender in addition to race and class.

Presentations in the media concerning the gender issues of popular culture have been widely discussed. The analytical field of research continues to be vast, and it establishes a common recurring theme that can be contradicted by individuals, but is widely performed by the masses. The following will review the theories and studies of several who have contributed to the examination of cultural ideals, images, and media representations.

Gender, Expectation, Ideals

The recognition of a woman is defined by a man's level of attraction (Berger 46). This is the stimulating force behind the predominant media interest in relation to gender and specifically, to women in society. Rita Freedman explains in her book, Beauty Bound, that this gender difference in physical attractiveness between men and women is widely accepted as a fact of nature (1). She further states:

The expectation of feminine beauty, inflates its importance, making women more vulnerable to 'lookism,' a stereotype similar to ageism or racism. Lookism is a form of social control that influences how people see themselves, and how they are seen by others (2).

In the widely acclaimed text <u>Ways of Seeing,</u> John Berger strengthens the analytical description of differences between the genders. Rosalind Coward supports Bergers' theories in her work, <u>Female Desires</u>. The western visual culture depends on the relationship between the image and the viewer. It is the expected role of the man to assume the controlling position in society, and demonstrate the continuous production of the male gaze. It is of crucial importance how a woman appears to a man, and the appreciation of herself is granted only by her acceptance from the dominant male. She now begins to graciously stand in the light of the eyes of men, and allow their watchful glance to measure and calculate her worth. "And so she comes to consider the surveyor and the surveyed within her as the two constituent yet always distinct elements of her identity as a woman" (Berger 46).

Coward adds to this by examining the male gaze as a camera, used to depict the mental ideal images as perceived by men. She states: "The camera in contemporary media has been put to use as an extension of the male gaze at women on the streets. Here, men can and do stare at women; men assess, judge, and make advances on the basis of these visual impressions" (75).

In modern society, looking is a natural practice. However, to look is to dominate. It is a critical aspect of human relations which establishes the positions of control and subordination.

Therefore, the woman in western society is a sight. She is a sight for the pleasures of men, constructed and driven by the ideals and desires of men. Her quest for acceptance is a continuous journey of creation, reconstruction, and conceptualization of beauty ideals, all of which will assist in the recognition of her place in society. In the text, <u>The Beauty Myth: How Images of Beauty Are Used Against Women</u>, Naomi Wolf explores how western women have escaped from "one form of enslavement into another." It discusses how the images and definitions of beauty limit women in every event of their lives. It states that "the beauty myth is always actually prescribing behavior and not appearance" (14). An advertisement for the fragrance "Cabriole," featured in the Elizabeth Arden cosmetic line, was presented in the text, <u>Consuming Passions: The Dynamics of Popular Culture</u> by Judith Williamson. It is a representation of the media implications of what it means to be a woman in Western society. The fragrance allows the woman to identify with not the modern female that she is today, but with the modern female that she must become tomorrow. The advertisement reads as follows:

> There is this woman. Watch her.....She is a tapestry of delicious contradictions. Capable of laughter that all the world may witness. And of

tears that no one will ever see. A swimmer who may never enter the water. A musician who may choose to listen rather than to play. A wife who feels like a lover. A mother who remembers what it was like to be a child. There is this woman. And here is the fragrance that defines her. We call it-Cabriole— because never before has there been a more rewarding time to be a woman (27).

Wolf also discusses the structure of the differences seen between the genders. She points out that men are one of the most imminent and powerful reasons that women yearn to be beautiful. Men have placed the limitations on appearance, and they know the essence of beauty that is desirable. Wolf also relates to the above mentioned concept that men calculate and measure a woman's worth in society, and that they have used women's "beauty" as a form of currency in circulation among other men.

These ideas about the definition of what is considered to be beautiful have continued to evolve throughout history side by side with ideas about money. Therefore, the two are seen as virtual parallels in our consumer economy. "A woman looks like a million dollars, she's a first-class beauty, her face is her fortune" (Wolf 20). To add to this theory, it can be simplified by returning to the original images and thoughts of Berger who stated that, "Men act, women appear. Men look at women. Women watch themselves being looked at" (47).

The attraction to the image of a woman's body, presented as an ideal form, is the natural response to the attraction of a pleasurable sight (Coward 77). Wolf continues by stating that the "culture alienates women from their own bodies and sexuality, and how little choice women really have about obsessions with appearance" (277). Wolf explores how women recognize the importance that they place on being beautiful, and that they are beginning to wonder if they aren't alone in this feeling, but that "something important is at stake that has to do with the relationship between female liberation and female beauty" (Wolf 9).

In addition, females are considered to be the "fair sex," however is there empirical evidence to suggest that this is true? Freedman poses the question, "What facts support the premise that beauty is gender bound?" The answer that she discovers is that "although few studies have specifically focused on beauty as a masculine or feminine trait, gender differences have emerged nevertheless." Research continues to indicate that "attitudes about attractiveness are applied differently to each sex. Beauty counts for everyone, but more so for women" (Freedman 9).

The Beauty Myth

What does it mean to be beautiful when being examined by the glare of the male gaze? "The beauty of a woman is naught but a delusion of the masculine brain clouded by the fumes of instinct" (Freedman 13). The word "beauty" contains a meaning that is complex yet simple. It is an outward appearance, a feeling, and a fact of social change. A woman who desires to be beautiful is trapped in the confines of the structured definition of what beauty should comprise.

Therefore, she consistently struggles with the complex, and continually attempts to master the grace of simplicity. The beauty myth is the cultivating extreme of the picture of women in society. It is this facade between the outward visual presence and the inner destruction that is created and reinforced by the culture and the media.

Myths help us to clarify perplexing events. They develop an understanding of what society forms as reality. Freedman explains that "cultures grow and mature as do children. Myths are to culture, what cognitive errors are to children's thought" (15). She further describes the relationship between myth and gender by stating:

> In fact, myths about gender, like myths about beauty, are often linked in just such counterbalanced pairs. Together, contrary myths create an equilibrium that helps preserve them both. Women are crowned with beauty precisely because they are cloaked in difference. The idealization of female appearance camouflages an underlying belief in female inferiority. Just as excessive narcissism has its roots in self-loathing, the myth of female beauty grows from the myth of female deviance. Beauty helps to balance

woman as a misbegotten person. It disguises her inadequacies and justifies her presence (18).

Wolf adds to this link between beauty and mythology by saying that "while culture works out of moral dilemmas, 'beauty' is amoral. From the beauties in male culture, women learn a bitter amoral lesson—that the moral lessons of their culture exclude them" (Wolf 59). Also, in the text Femininity, author Susan Brownmiller states that "women in our society are forced daily to compete for male approval, enslaved by ludicrous beauty standards that we ourselves are conditioned to take seriously and to accept" (25).

In contradiction to this "beauty myth," Karen Lehrman, in her book The Lipstick Proviso, explains that if a woman is not considered to be beautiful in society, she will be labeled as "deficient, defective, a failure" (66). These are extreme words that women have come to use to describe themselves if they do not meet a certain cultural standard. Lehrman analyzes Wolf's concept of the "beauty myth," and what she comes to realize is that "beauty is not a myth, an arbitrary cultural convention, an ideological fabrication. Beauty is a reality, a gift of God, nature, or genius that, to some extent, transcends culture and history" (68).

However, she does continue in support of the previously stated theories, and points out that although different cultures and eras have emphasized different features and body types, the common thread is that physical beauty is of the highest importance. The female body is acclaimed for its appeal. Again, Brownmiller adds to the established premise by saying, "exalted by poets, painters, and sculptors, the female body, often reduced to its isolated parts, has been mankind's most popular subject for adoration and myth, and also for judgement, ridicule, esthetic alteration, and violent abuse" (27). Due to this, "women's desire to obtain attractiveness is buried deep within their psyches" (Lehrman 69).

"A woman's worthiness is equated with her beauty," and this concept of "worth" relates back to Wolf's discussion of women being placed in comparison to the measurement and calculation witnessed by men in popular culture. In addition, Lehrman discusses the various ways that women, while striving to meet the images of beauty, adopt to become accepted and adored. She states:

> In the name of beauty, women have crippled their feet, broken their ribs, inflated their breasts, deflated their thighs, and lifted their faces and rears. They have fainted from corsets too tight, fallen from heels too high, developed cancer from too much sun, died from two little food—often to find that the ideal that they were trying to achieve had been revised (66).

What can be witnessed in this society is that women are judged more critically for outward appeal, and they are rejected more severely when it is lacking. Therefore, Freedman states that a "woman's beauty is constantly anticipated, encouraged, sought, and rewarded in a wide range of situations" (10). She continues by saying that a cosmetic alteration performed by the hand of an anxious woman helps to transform her into the acceptable. Aristotle wrote that "beauty is a greater recommendation than any letter of introduction." Freedman concurs with this statement, and she describes the modern, womanly perspective that is all too common. She states:

> Women's efforts to reshape their image are entangled with their efforts to reshape the world. Feminine beauty is so readily rewarded that it becomes enmeshed with other motives — for mastery, for security, for self-esteem. Adornment and achievement are two ends of a seesaw that females ride as they seek to balance their need for love with their need for work. Pushing high toward one end, they are too often judged for the other. Swinging down again, they collide with their own ambitions as well as with their own ambivalence (98).

Culture Control

As stated in the text, Understanding Media Cultures: Social Theory and Mass Communication, Nick Stevenson illustrates his definition of culture that places the issues of gender, society, and idealization into perspective. It is as follows: "Culture is an intersubjectively produced, publicly held phenomenon. It helps provide a source of identity, means of social exchange and a sense of community" (47).

In the article, "Understanding Popular Culture," the author states that "culture is the constant process of producing meanings of and from our social experience, and such meanings necessarily produce a social identity for the people involved" (Fiske 2). In addition, the article "Commodities and Culture," adds to this definition by saying that popular culture is created by the people, not produced by the culture industry. "By 'the people' it is the shifting set of social allegiances, which are described better in terms of people's felt collectivity than in terms of external sociological factors such as gender, age, race, and region" (Fiske 24).

It is the standard within this cultural composition that the ideas of gender and dominance are produced and maintained. From this series of male behavior and desire which create the cultural ideal that women strive to achieve, an ideology develops that may only be contested or acquired, the latter being the favored choice. "The study of ideology can be usefully defined as the ways in which meaning (signification) serves to sustain relations of domination" (Stevenson 86). Therefore, it is within this system of beliefs that formulate and validate the established position of womanly standards.

Those who contradict that the advancements of modern society have returned the control of women to their rightful owners, will only be met with an overwhelming disbelief. Michelle Zimbalist Rosaldo in her text entitled, Woman, Culture, and Society, states that, "Women may be important, powerful, and influential, but it seems that, relative to men of their age and social status, women everywhere lack generally recognized and culturally valued authority" (17). Again, this is saying that women relinquish their personal control to men at the expense of their acceptance. Therefore, the feminist approach to regaining ownership over their female presence in popular culture is an active reform.

Feminist Findings

"Feminism is utopian to the extent to which it bases an imaginary politics on the future possibility of living in a world where no men no longer dominate women" (Stevenson 104). Brownmiller states:

> The aim is not to propose a definition of femininity, one that better suits the coming decade or one that lays claim to moral (or physical) superiority as some sort of intrinsic female province, but to invite examination of a compelling esthetic and the reasons for its perseverance, in the effort to illuminate the restrictions on free choice (235).

Brownmiller continues by discussing the ways in which a woman feels when she is accepted based on her physical appearance. She believes that it is a stroke of anatomical luck, or an accident of genetics that physical characteristics would fall within the idealized norm (172).

Lehrman states that "feminist theory has never been monolithic." However, it appears that for the past quarter century a number of closely related feminist beliefs have dominated both academic and popular writing on the subject of women. Lehrman also adds that "according to this set of beliefs, the reason all women haven't turned into liberated women is that the 'patriarchy,' typically defined as a pervasive and self-sustaining system of male domination and privilege, stands resolutely in the way" (9). Clearly the many changes that have occurred during the quest to accomplish women's goals, behaviors and demeanors during the past thirty years confirm a vast portion of the feminist argument: "the traditional notion of femininity has been strongly shaped by cultural norms" (Lehrman 39).

Women have an undesirable level of self-esteem and self-worth which is formulated by the representations of the media, the male controlled culture, and the societal standards. Freedman adds to this by asking, "What motivates females to transform themselves?" She finds that the answer is that there is a strong need to conform to social norms. "Women enact the popular image for the pleasure of being like others and of being liked by others"(Freedman 48).

As feminists approach the issues of beauty, they reach conclusions that resound in agreement. They recognize the beauty mystique and the constrainment that women perceive as natural. The progression of the feminist movement has been positive, yet the power of the popular culture and the media interest that fortifies the ideals, have remained supreme. Wolf writes that one of the media's most damaging lies is that "beauty can be earned by any woman through hard work and enterprise." Lehrman finds such a claim to be untrue. She feels that Wolf ignores the most important point: there is no reason why women should not believe that through some enterprise, they can make themselves more attractive (78). However, Wolf retaliates this belief with her statement that "a cultural fixation is not an obsession about female beauty but an obsession about female obedience" (Lehrman 83). Therefore, enterprise is not required unless told to do so.

Lehrman explains that despite such apparent progress, many feminists claim that the beauty ideal is not merely a cultural fixation with destructive side effects. Rather it is a patriarchal ploy used to both control women sexually and morally, and to earn profits for male dominance (68). "The more progress that women make, the argument now goes, the more society has forced women to abide by an increasingly strict and restrictive beauty ideal" (Lehrman 68). In addition, in the article, "Photography Review: Beauty, in a Variety of Guises," Sarah Boxer examines a woman's appearance and her strive for ultimate perfection. She also describes the belief within women that unless they meet a certain criteria of beauty, they are considered to be nonexistent in society.

Also, Brownmiller states that, "The great paradox of femininity, is that a judicious concession here and there has been known to work wonders as protective coloration in a man's world and as a means of survival, but total surrender has stopped women point-blank from major forms of achievement" (235). Finally, Brownmiller recognizes the competitive capacity of women to reach their beauty goals. She states that "the conflicts that are rife in ladylike refinement, a submissive demeanor and dazzling allure guarantee that women will be divided among themselves, suspicious of other women as they seek to master an impossible formula to win the approval of men" (Brownmiller 236).

The author Tracy Quan, believes that "intelligent femininity is a delicate art, balancing self-indulgence with self-discipline" (Chamberlain 59). Wolf agrees to this, and she advocates "power feminism" to replace "victim feminism." She further states that, "while it is important to reexamine the assumptions of early feminism in the light of social change, it seems that with the exception of a few women who are usually privileged economically and psychologically, we as a society, are far from free" (Chamberlain 60). Further, Martha T. McCluskey concurs to this when she wrote, "We each share a complicated and contextual mixture of identity of privilege and oppression" (Chamberlain 62).

The Barbie Image

The author M.G. Lord has been recognized as the most acclaimed writer on the analysis of the Barbie doll. In her text, <u>Forever Barbie</u>, she has situated herself within the image of an ideal. Lord states that "Barbie may be the most potent icon of American popular culture in the late twentieth century" (Lord 6).

She has captivated women in many ways, and Lord examines the perception of cultural acceptance of the Barbie doll. One important point to note is that this writer discusses that Barbie is more than a representation of what is considered to be "beautiful." Lord states, "She didn't teach us to nurture, she taught us independence. Barbie was her own woman. She could invent herself with a costume change. She was Grace Slick and Sally Ride, Marie Osmond and Marie Curie. She was all that we could be" (Lord 9). And at the same time, she was a representation of a physical image that we could never become.

Jill Barad is the current chief executive officer of the Mattel corporation who works exclusively with the promotion and development of the Barbie doll. When Lord asked her if she was a feminist, she replied, "I don't know what that means. There are negative implications and positive implications. I believe that there are many dimensions to being a woman" (Berens 4).

Many others have taken part of the critique against the Barbie doll. For example, Jane Sarasohn-Kahn in her book, <u>Contemporary Barbie Dolls 1980 and</u>

Beyond, explores the many developments of the Barbie doll, and how women have changed and grown with her evolution. In the article "Idollatry" by Kathy Chamberlain, the Barbie doll is seen as a symbol of sexism for many feminists. The Barbie doll has become part of the American psyche and it sets unrealistic standards for the female body.

In addition, this piece states that, "Over the years, despite the successes of the woman's movement, Barbie has proliferated wildly, making only cosmetic accommodations to feminist sensibilities" (Chamberlain 57). This article also explains that the book "Forever Barbie, by M.G. Lord, while full of lore an analysis, is not sufficiently critical of the toy as a purveyor of negative concepts of women" (Chamberlain 58).

Further, to continue this analysis, the article "Ken and Barbie at Life Size: Sex Roles a Journal of Research," the writer Kevin Norton describes the considerable discussion in both the scientific literature and the general media concerning the appropriateness of the body shape and proportions of the Barbie doll. The concern has been about the possible influence that this doll has had over women, and how they perceive their bodies in comparison to the doll. It appears that her shape is the "cultural ideal."

Norton continues by discussing that the Barbie image "may create mental depictions of what is to be expected later in life including gender, ethnic stereotypes and body image. A major representation of the body are dolls, which are socially acceptable, intensively advertised, almost universal, and have the immediacy of a tactile presence" (287).

The creator of the Barbie doll, Ruth Handler, remarked that Barbie who was designed in 1959, has become a "symbol of womanhood." Handler has seen her creation grow from "hunch to hit to controversial icon." In the article "A Doll's Life," Handler also describes the adult fascination with the Barbie doll. "Thousands of women around the world consider themselves to be serious collectors, including one who recently paid $17,000 for a rare prototype, the highest price ever paid for a Barbie doll. There are annual Barbie conventions and a magazine, "Barbie Bazaar," with a monthly circulation of more than 20,000" (Groves 8). This is just some of the ways to measure the importance of this doll in women's lives.

The image of Barbie is an extreme power. In the article, "How Cindy Got Her Revenge on Men," Corinna Honan depicts the life of one woman, Cindy Jackson, who took the image of Barbie very personally. She has created a living version of the Barbie doll— herself. Jackson has had numerous operations to look like the doll because she feels that it is the ultimate way *How so?* to get revenge on men. Now, she is inspiring others to do the same. She chose the Barbie doll as the consummate model of a woman. To her, it is the face of power, and she cannot rest until this face is what she sees as her reflection.

Therefore, the way that women relate to these cultural ideals, achieving a match to the "perfect" standard of an image such as the Barbie doll, illuminates the damaging path to acceptance that they begin to follow. Coward once again explains a critical detail concerning the relationship between woman, personal image, and cultural ideal. She states:

> Over the mirror always hangs the image of the socially approved, massively consumed, widely circulated image of the generic Woman. She alone it seems is guaranteed an easy ride through life, guaranteed the approval of all and safe in expecting uncritical love. Only she is guaranteed to recapture that happy childhood state, where child and adults alike gloried in the child's image" (80).

The eyes of a child perceive the doll as a symbol of their imagination; the eyes of a woman perceive the doll as a symbol of the male gaze. The image-obsessed culture, created and reinforced by the media, shouts forth a controlling command to warn women not to lose their recognition in society. "And through this command to meet the ideal, our society writes one message loud and clear across the female body: Do not act. Do not desire. Wait for men's attention" —And they continue to do so (Coward 82).

"Barbie Doll" By Marge Piercy
Selected from the Piercy collection.

The following is a poem based on the feminist beliefs of author Marge Piercy who finds the Barbie doll as a representation of a destructive ideal.

This girlchild was born as usual
and presented dolls that did pee-pee
and miniature GE stoves and irons
and wee lipsticks the color of cherry candy.
Then in the magic of puberty, a classmate said:
You have a great big nose and fat legs.

She was healthy, tested intelligent,
possessed strong arms and back,
abundant sexual drive and manual dexterity
She went to and fro apologizing.
Everyone saw a fat nose on thick legs.

She was advised to play coy,
exhorted to come on hearty,
exercise, diet, smile and wheedle.
Her good nature wore out
like a fan belt.
So she cut off her nose and her legs
and offered them up.

In the casket displayed on satin she lay
with the undertaker's cosmetics painted on,
a turned-up putty nose,
dressed in a pink and white nightie.

Doesn't she look pretty? Everyone said.
Consummation at last.
To every woman a happy ending.

The vivid expression of this poem paints an unpleasant picture in the minds of women, however it is one which is a part of an intricate reality. It is the analysis of a girl, who was told from the delicate point in her youth, about each of her physical imperfections. She did not meet the cultural representation of a "beautiful" image. Her intelligence, health, and strength were not recognized as important or valuable. Rather, she was forced to transform her outside, while she slowly lost the identity of her consciousness on the inside.

Piercy's poem, which appeared in 1969, sends the same message now as it did in the distant past. In order for a woman to achieve a sense of self, a sense of worth, or a sense of acceptability in American society, she must adhere to the policy that to be beautiful is to be recognized. And when a woman strives so passionately to accomplish beauty, why would she ever want to be invisible?

Consuming Money and Mind

As an image is represented within the context of popular culture, the members of that society begin to take on the role of consumer. They delve into the materialism of the mass market, and attempt to identify with the image of the icon that is considered as ideal. Consumers on a quest to reach the perfected standard, use their values to help determine the importance of goods and services that bring them to the expected level of acceptance. This type of consumer who identifies with a cultural image or iconic presence in society, is described as being aesthetically oriented. Therefore, those that desire the Barbie image, are people who seek out and focus on the connection of their perceptions and experiences.

Robert Settle in his text, <u>Why They Buy:</u> <u>American Consumers Inside and Out</u>, states:

> Those who dearly value beauty are most often directed to the symmetry and form of the objects in their environment. They're likely to value and respect the artistic episodes and experiences of life and hold beauty and charm as more desirable than correctness and accuracy, as an intellectual would, or utility and potency, as would a pragmatic materialist. These consumers may also equate truth with beauty or confuse peak sensory experiences with the purely spiritual elevation of consciousness (55).

In addition, consumers go through an eight step process which motivates them to achieve the desirable image and ideal. The steps are as follows: exposition, stimulation, sensation, attention, perception, retention, recollection, and application (Settle 71).

Williamson describes the perception of a "consuming passion" which envelops consumers as they aspire to accomplish the goals as presented by the mass media. It is a damaging series of events which continues to taunt the minds of the popular culture. Williamson states: "Consuming passions can mean many things: an all-embracing passion, a passion for consumerism. The concern is the way that passions are themselves consumed, contained and channeled into the very social structures they might otherwise threaten" (11).

The Barbie Image: A New Perspective

The preceding review of analytical works in the fields of mass media, popular culture, and femininity, have addressed the image of the Barbie doll. However, this doll has been placed mainly within the context of body image and stereotypical representations. It has been examined as an archetype for children, and as a feature for discussions of femininity. However, the following study will not focus on the relation of children to the doll, nor will it analyze the physical characteristics as a reality for the modern female. Rather, this study will formulate the position of the Barbie image within the perfected ideal as portrayed by popular culture and the mass media. It will also assess the connection of the implemented ideal to the practice of marketing and consumerism.

Women, striving to achieve the answers to the beauty mythology, often find that the image that they have known as familiar and perceived as beautiful, is the reproduction of a doll recognizable to all. Therefore, this study will address the ways in which women place themselves into the representation of the Barbie doll, and the achievement of the doll's success and importance within the media, market, and popular culture.

Chapter Three
Methodology

Model Methods

The methodology that is used for this thesis is a cultural analysis which critically interprets the issue of the Barbie doll as an idealized icon. This form of study, reflected in the work of scholars such as Stuart Hall, exemplifies the "use of media material as evidence of how some ways of thinking are socially 'privileged' over others, and identifies the media as an instrument through which this is accomplished" (Hornig Priest 54). Therefore, it examines a premier set of ideological beliefs, and the cultural critique allows for the evaluation of images and representations seen as prominent within society.

what is this?

The design for this method is similar to the work of Ramona Curry in her publication, Too Much of a Good Thing: Mae West as Cultural Icon. This work explores the altering figurations of the image of Mae West in twentieth century popular culture. It examines West's iconography as two separate and distinct images within society, showing both the respectability of the image as a role-model, and the negative feministic implications. Curry not only analyzes the "symbolic roles West has occupied, arguing that the entertainer represents a carefully orchestrated transgression of race, class, and gender expectations, she also illustrates how icons of pop culture often distill contested social issues, serving diverse and even contradictory political functions" (30).

Star studies have emphasized the ways in which different members of society have appropriated star images. The studies have analyzed their meanings in relation to the dominant ideology. As Curry examines the identity of this figure as an icon, she also explores the changing meaning of that icon. Therefore, she evaluates "how 'Mae West' has functioned for much of the twentieth century as a sign, what the sign has signified in the past, and how and what it represents currently" (Robertson 61).

Curry takes the reader through the study chronologically. However, there are an evident amount of time gaps, which is explained by the fact that Curry is interested in West as an icon, and not in presenting a biographical account of the star's history or career. In her investigation of West's image, "Curry combines a rich variety of methodologies — industrial and social histories, genre studies, close textual readings, cultural studies, and feminist-inflected psychoanalytic criticism" (Robertson 63).

This thesis also features an additional study which parallels the exploration of the statement of objectives. In this instance, the consumerism of an icon is examined. Again, the design of Curry's study serves as a model for this analysis. Curry discusses that most consumers still recognize West as the iconic image, are familiar with several of her popular cinematic lines, and can enjoy parodies and imitations of the "star." Therefore, Curry analyzes promotional materials, critical texts, censorship documents, and other public images as witnessed in the media. Each of these aspects provide the insight into the various, sometimes competing, public discourses about West, and how they have evolved over time (Robertson 62). To further illustrate this element within the thesis, Curry states:

> My position that the icon "Mae West" has diverse though structured meanings that have emerged through its historical circulation entails an understanding that popular culture consumers are themselves producers. These "coproducing" consumers jointly and variably ascribe meanings to a cultural sign nominally fashioned by material producers of American mass culture (xviii).

The main theme and concept of this thesis is achieved through the examination of the issues of femininity, and the representations and characteristics of an icon. In the model study, it was analyzed by the perception of Curry, and in this analysis, it is presented through the personal perception of a member of popular culture who has witnessed, researched, and lived within the female perspective. Femininity represents the balance of critical thought in support or opposition to the representation of women in Western society, and how they identify with these images. It also depicts the ideals women attempt to obtain, and how consumerism and the mass media create and nurture these needs and ideals.

The image of an icon must be analyzed in a multi-level fashion so that the contributing elements are recognized. Understanding the development of an icon, can be achieved when one perceives the ideals presented in the mass media and mass market as being influential to the creation of the image. Curry addresses "Mae West" from three intertwined perspectives: first, as a singular case history revealing how star images emerge and circulate as cultural signs; second, as a social phenomenon that played a central role in the establishment of cultural politics; and third, as a site at which the interrogation and development of critical media theories of gender representations about the "spectacle, excess, and parody that constitute masquerade" are expressed (xv).

In the "Introduction" of the volume, Curry states that she "argues for a historical understanding of popular signs as dynamic constructions in relation to specific audiences and issues in the public sphere" (xvi). Therefore, the study illustrates how stars, celebrities, or icons symbolize meanings in cultural context by interpreting in detail what the image has signified.

In addition, in the text Stars by Richard Dyer, he also examines the identity of star culture, and the issues of appeal, acceptance, and manipulation of the public. Individuals begin to adhere to the behavioral classifications of the star-audience relationship. Dyer explores their emotional affinity to the icon, self-identification, imitation, and projection. It is the separation from the "real-world" and the connection to the "star-world." The author also examines the importance of beauty for the star. He states, "One function a star serves is to fix a type of beauty, to help a physical type identify itself" (16).

Similar evaluations have also been presented in the field of cultural studies that analyze the transformation of an image to an icon in popular culture, and the characteristics they possess that enable this transformation to take place. The text Superman at Fifty, edited by Dennis Dooley and Gary Engle, examines the representation of the hero in society as the "persistence of a legend."

The authors state that "We are a nation rich with legendary figures. Superman achieves truly mythic stature, interweaving a pattern of beliefs, literary conventions and cultural traditions of the American people more powerfully and more accessibly that any other cultural symbol of the twentieth century, perhaps of any period in our history"(80). The design of this study looks at the cultural implications of the image of Superman, and examines the characteristics such as strength, mobility, and extrasensory power, that fortify the identification and appeal of this image.

Dooley and Engle believe that the image of "Superman" has been culturally adored and accepted among the host of comic-book characters with ease. The personal qualities of Superman are the comic-book equivalents of ethnic characteristics. The authors state that the ideals of the image "protect and preserve the vitality of the foster community in which he lives in the same way that immigrant ethnicity has sustained American culture linguistically, artistically, economically, politically and spiritually"(81). Therefore, the image of Superman has maintained the core of the American myth that has been idealized within Western society.

A supporting study which reflects the marketing analysis of this thesis is the depiction of Lara Croft, a computer-generated action heroine, in the article, "Lara Croft, the Bit Girl: How a Game Star Became a '90's Icon." She is described by author Jane Hughes, as the "icy, sexy, British aristocrat and adventure-seeking archaeologist."After her appearance in the computer-animated game "Tomb Raider," she has assisted in selling nearly 3 million copies, has become a popular icon in demand for a large quantity of other promotional uses, and has been the subject of 100 Internet sites (Hughes 82).

The character has created a media phenomenon, and the issues of femininity are based on the concept of sexuality and physical dimensions. The inventor of Croft states that, "If you can create a great character, what you have is a franchise" (Hughes 83). The critique of Croft's image analyzes her in the perspective of an icon in popular culture. It examines her appeal, her marketability, and her success. It demonstrates how members of Western society fixate on an image, and make it an intricate piece of their reality. In addition, the relation of the person to the image as being a unique encounter of values and perception is made evident: "The interaction is between the player and Lara; it is a very personal experience" (Hughes 84).

Dyer also discusses the evaluation of stars as a "phenomenon of production." The idea presented is that stars are images which are products of Hollywood, in the same way that icons are images which are products of the culture. "Perspective stars are seen in terms of their function in the economy of Hollywood, including, crucially, their role in the manipulation of Hollywood's market, the audience" (10). Stars are widely regarded as a vital element in the economics of Hollywood in terms of: capital, investment, outlay, and the market (Dyer 11).

The icon is a representation of society. They serve to disguise the fact that they are produced images, and constructed personalities. "Thus the value embodied by a star is as it were harder to reject as 'impossible' or 'false,' because the star's existence guarantees the existence of the value he or she embodies" (Dyer 22). Therefore, the present thesis follows a methodology of cultural examination and critical interpretation, and the significant issues of the analysis are the following representations.

The Barbie doll is an image which has formed as a cultural icon, and has been highly recognized for forty years. She has been studied as a damaging symbol to young females, and has been placed within the context of femininity, beauty ideals, and gender roles. However, her representation in the mass media has been limited to a discussion concerning unrealistic body proportions and feministic implications.

The focus of this analysis examines and explores the importance of the Barbie doll in American society. It analyzes the doll on the basis of the characteristic of "respectability" which the Barbie image was created, and has strived to maintain. It interprets the Barbie doll as an icon in popular culture, and the values and morality of the women who identify with her image. It allows a discovery to unfold as her detailed and personal meaning within them takes form.

Why has the Barbie doll continued to be successful for over four decades? What is it that causes women to join the vast array of adult collectors, consume and contribute to the printed material available on shelves or online, or reconstruct their physical appearance to resemble the ideal features of the delicate designer toy? The study that follows achieves answers to the preceding questions, and provides an understanding to the widespread attention and interest that this doll has continued to generate. It is an interpretation of many factors that have influenced the Barbie image such as femininity, character, and marketing insight, and demonstrates their contribution to the ever-changing Barbie paradigm.

Definition of Terms

- *Barbie Image* — The Barbie image in popular culture is a representation of an ideal female. In Western society, both women and men perceive her to be comprised of two distinct elements: physical object and invented personality. She is either criticized or she is adored. Therefore, "at one moment her beauty is coveted as an asset; the next moment it may be shunned as a liability" (Freedman 5).

- *Beauty*— As defined in the text, Beauty Bound, the author Rita Freedman defined beauty as "an external radiance and inner tranquility, a sexual

50

allure, a fact of social exchange" (4).

- **_Beauty Myth_** — Beauty Myth is a term that was presented in the text, The Beauty Myth, by the author Naomi Wolf. In this text, Wolf explains that this myth tells a story that comprises the quality of "beauty" which is universally recognized. Wolf describes that "women must want to embody it, and men must want to possess women who embody it"(12). Further, the analysis of the myth is that a woman's beauty must correspond to her fertility, and Wolf states that "since this system is based on sexual selection, it is inevitable and changeless" — none of this is said to be true (12).

- **_Commodity_** — Commodities have both cultural and functional values. The concept of the economy is not one of money, rather it is one of meanings and pleasures which constitute a major resource of popular culture. In the article "Commodities and Culture," the author defines this term by stating that, "In this economy there are no consumers, only circulators of meanings, for meanings are the only elements in the process that can be neither commodified nor consumed: meanings can be produced, reproduced, and circulated only in that constant process that we call culture" (Fiske 27).

- **_Cultural Icon_** — A cultural icon is an image

which is highly recognized, replicated, or analyzed within a society. The Barbie doll is a cultural icon for contemporary Western civilization.

- *Femininity/Feminism* — Karen Lehrman, in her text <u>The Lipstick Proviso</u>, critically analyzes the field of research concerning femininity. She defines feminism as "Not a set of commands, but a set of challenges. It represents an ideal to which not only society, but women themselves must aspire" (201). Femininity is the most critical aspect for the basis of this study. Therefore, the author Susan Brownmiller in her text entitled <u>Femininity</u>, presents a thorough definition which has been used as the primary theory for this analysis. She begins by saying that femininity is a "nostalgic tradition of imposed limitations" (14). Femininity thrives on the premise that there is a need to please men, and the competitive nature of women is released as they attempt to secure men. Femininity always demands more, constantly reassuring its audience by a willing demonstration of difference (Brownmiller 15).

- *Popular Culture* — Popular culture is created by the people within society. It is not produced or imposed upon them by the culture industry. The article "Commodities and Culture" adds that "popular culture is made by the people at the interface between the products of the culture industries and everyday life" (Fiske 24).

Chapter Four
Discussion Part One:
Cultural Analysis

The Image in the Mirror

A reflection of society, and a response to popular culture, the image of an icon is the image in the mirror. The mirror that creates a presence for the representations of all that society claims as ideal in the likeness of the viewer. In Western society, images within the culture are idolized or criticized, and through the transformations of the decades, one legend continues to prevail. She is a vision of a paradigm, an object of desire, and a controversial preference. She is the Barbie doll.

The revered success and imagery of the Barbie doll has been analyzed and explored throughout the passing of time. However, there is still a vast portion of knowledge and discovery to be found within the depths of this petite figure with a wealth of implications. In 1959, the year of her creation, Barbie filled a void within society. She established a position that demonstrated her ability to captivate the market. Today, this model image continues to dominate the culture, but the power of the Barbie doll rests in her passion for change.

As an institution in United States doll culture, Barbie does not remain static. She is made to adapt, to improve and to expand. The author M.G. Lord stated that "Barbie may be the most potent icon in American culture in the late twentieth century. She is an archetypal female figure, something upon which young girls and women project their idealized selves" (Groves 10). Therefore, women have been performing this practice for forty years, and this has been made possible because the Barbie doll has mastered the art of alterations. She has conformed to society, yet has continued to mark her place as an icon of Western civilization. Static she is not, however, "in a world shot through with uncertainty she is an island of stability"(Riddick 1).

As the continual reinvention of the Barbie doll occurs, the admiration and identification with this symbol has never lost intensity. Women compare their personal image to less than that of a one-foot mold of plastic. This is a common element within popular culture because society has named Barbie as a standard. She is a standard of beauty, perfection, and ideology. Barbie defies that she is a doll in the subconscious of society, rather, she appears in the mind as an actual being. She is comprised of two main components: physical object and invented personality (Lord 4). We discuss and create fantasy for her in hopes that she will materialize and speak to us as if she has been dearly familiar all of our lives. In fact, she simply has.

Feminists may argue against her representations, but no individual can deny that she has been successfully present for over four decades, and the reason for her triumph lies strictly within ourselves. For many, she is the vision projected into the mirror. Barbie has both shaped and responded to the expectations of the marketplace, and she is a reflection of the values of the American popular culture.

Respect is a Beautiful Thing

To be respectable is to fulfill an image. It is to identify with what society deems as admirable — to be hard working in an honorable occupation, to be an upstanding member of society, and to strive to accomplish what you believe. These characteristics are created by the ideals of popular culture. They existed in the year 1959, and remain accurate in 1999.

Appearing to be desirable qualities, the mentioned characteristics are representations of the middle class. Therefore, in recognition of this image, the creators of the Barbie doll designed an icon of "respectability." It was the primary goal of the Mattel corporation to maintain the standard of the Barbie image. In an ever-changing world, the adaptation of Barbie could persist, but her quest to be respectable could never be tainted. She was formed as a member of the middle class, however as her identity strengthens, does she continue to reside in the minds and hearts of this class as an image of respectability, or as one of beauty? In addition, is she a reflection of this characteristic in the "respectable" values of society?

In 1959, a wave of phenomenon spread throughout the Western world like a fire that illuminated the interest within females to identify with the Barbie doll. She quickly provided the initial recognition of an adult doll who exuded independence. As her popularity increased, she became a figure that young girls desired to emulate, and Barbie was earning a significant amount of original respectability. She was more than a fashion model, and the world was her runway. She portrayed success in many careers, and always made it possible to do each with the essence of glamour. Ruth Handler had wanted the dream-weavers of Barbie to create a unique personality for the doll, and allow her to continually become the product of their imagination. However, it was soon evidenced that Barbie was accepting and molding an identity of her own.

As Barbie emerged into the nineties, she reigned and continues to dominate to the theme of "We girls can do anything." She has made an abundance of occupations appear enchanting, and her respectability through the perception of Mattel, remains untouched. As her reformation overcomes the boundaries of the marketplace, the surface image of respectability seems to continue as a prevalent detail. However, as the image of the Barbie doll is interpreted further, her ideal characteristic may prove to be questionable.

It has been stated previously, and reiterated throughout various facets of popular culture, that the standards of beauty control and consume the lives of contemporary society. The culture responds to images of attraction. A pleasing appearance commands attention and the need to surround our environment with a series of "beautiful" and idealized objects. Barbie is categorically placed within this careful realm of objectivity. Mattel is aware of their degree of control when presenting the figure of a doll that is considered to be beautiful and appealing to both women and to men. Therefore, the immediate attention is intricately focused on the features of the doll, the designer fashions, and the delicate accessories, and not on the recognition that Barbie has assumed the respectable role of a doctor or a dentist. She is only desired in this image and capacity when she appears as a beautiful specimen, complete with the perfected glow of a cover model. The values of the Barbie doll are reflected by the conceptions of the creators, who are reflecting the conceptions of the culture in which they live.

Therefore, the values that Barbie possess are overshadowed by the obsession with her proportions. She upholds the precedence of respectability in her choice of occupations and "All-American" girl demeanor, but it appears that her values for the respectability as a representation of the middle class are becoming altered. If it is true that Barbie was created in 1959 within the construction of the middle class, and accepts the credo that "she's one of us," why is it that in 1999, Barbie is living an opulent, illusionary life of luxury?

Today, Barbie enjoys the fashions of designer labels such as Ralph Lauren, Bob Mackie, and Christian Dior. They are named as the most sophisticated Barbie dolls ever made. However, if Barbie is continuing an image created for her in 1959 that was one of the representations of the middle class, than we should not be receiving the message that one is never too young or too old to become an elitist. The intention of the Barbie doll was to be a respectable fantasy for young girls, not the image of glamour and beauty that women need to attain and men continue to desire. She has assumed a membership in a higher level of class, and the representation of her values are adjusting to the ideas of respectability as created by the popular culture.

In addition to these features, the amount of media interest and importance placed on the Barbie doll questions the respectability of those within society who have analyzed her image. The effect of the doll causes widespread attention. When the announcement was made concerning the creation of the new-dimensional Barbie, which will be addressed later in the thesis, the author Gloria Borger stated that she was "all set to write something about Iraq when a headline on the front page of the Wall Street Journal trumpeted some news not to be disregarded: 'Top-Heavy Barbie Is Getting Body Work" (Borger 40). What is wrong with the values and respectability of society that they find global affairs of lesser importance than the physical construction of a plastic doll? Again, the popular culture finds its focus on image, not on the substance of value, and again, the identity of Barbie goes beyond independence and reaches the nadir of idealism.

A final social commentary on the issues of respectability and value that is prevalent within the mass media concerning the Barbie doll during her introduction in 1959 and in her current existence, would be her appearance in musical representations. The following will present the lyrics of two musical compilations which represent the identity and image of the Barbie doll: the original Barbie theme from 1959, and the recently released track "Barbie Girl" performed by the Danish musical talent "Aqua."

Original Barbie Doll Theme

Barbie, you're beautiful
You make me feel
My Barbie doll is really real.

Barbie small and so petite
The clothes and figure look so neat.

Her dazzling outfit rings a bell
At parties she will cast a spell.

Someday I'm gonna be
Exactly like you
'Til then I know just what I'll do.

"Barbie Girl"

Hi Barbie
Hi Ken
Do you wanna go for a ride?
Sure Ken..
Jump in..

I'm a Barbie girl, in a Barbie world
Life in plastic, it's fantastic.
You can brush my hair, undress me everywhere.
Imagination, life is your creation.
Come on Barbie, let's go party!

I'm a blond little girl, in a fantasy world
Dress me up, make it tight, I'm your darling.
You are my doll, rock 'n' roll, feel the glamouring thing
Kiss me here, touch me there, hanky panky.
You can touch, you can play, if you say: "I'm always yours."

(Repeat chorus)

Make me walk, make me talk, do whatever you please
I can act like a star, I can beg on my knees.
Come jump in, be my friend, let us do it again
Hit the town, fool around, let's go party
You can touch, you can play, if you say: "I'm always yours."

In contemporary Western society, the level of information that can be determined about image and ideology demonstrated through music is significantly high. Music can portray the visions of popular culture, and the expression of ideas and representations within society. In each of the above pieces, the imagery of the Barbie doll is reflected by the composers of the song. It is their constructed conception of Barbie that takes form, and it is an outward assertion of her presence within society during each of these times.

The original theme song from 1959 focuses on the appearance of the doll, and the exceptional capacity for her to allow the owner to praise and emulate her. If the primary intention of the Barbie doll is to appear as respectable, independent, and value-filled, it is striking to review the lyrics and discover that the only focus concerns a "dazzling outfit," a "petite figure," and due to her beauty, she will enigmatically "cast a spell."

The song also begins and ends with the owner of the doll perceiving Barbie as a valid image with human characteristics, and establishes the desire within females to set out on a hopeful journey to become a replica of this depiction. In addition, the song concludes by saying, "'Til then I know just what I'll do." However, what is it that Mattel, society, or the image of Barbie is telling females to do? The implication is not to be respectable and continue the focus on values as it is claimed, rather, to become beautiful, stay slender, and maintain the height of fashion.

The second example is the song "Barbie Girl" that was released as a social commentary on the subject of the Barbie doll. The release was met with a flourish of interest, placing it as number nine on Billboard's Hot 100 singles chart. However, Mattel fiercely protected Barbie's image by claiming that the lyrics of the song "associate sexual and other unsavory themes with Mattel's Barbie products." Therefore, the Mattel corporation seeks trial on nine specific counts including "trademark infringement, false description, and wrongful use of a registered mark and unfair competition" (Crawford 1).

It is the "respectability" of the Barbie doll image that is being defended and upheld, however, the culture is creating an unparalleled identity. Examining the lyrics, it is evident that the image of beauty and superficiality is again prevalent. The song speaks of "a

Barbie girl in a Barbie world," where one needs to fulfill the fantasy of being blond, little, and plastic. Also, due to societal change, the appearance of the male image "Ken" is now represented, and was not proposed in the original theme. The Ken figure assumes a role of dominance as Barbie addresses him to "make her walk, make her talk, do whatever you please." The appearance of this element within the lyrics is a representation that men desire the image of the ideal, and the position of control.

Therefore, when exploring the ideology of value and respectability in the realm of the Barbie doll, a conclusion can be made. Barbie may have been created in 1959 with the distinguishing characteristic of "respectability" as found in the middle class. However, as time proceeds, the culture progresses and Barbie follows. The difficulty is separating the two components that comprise her identity: Barbie as physical object, and Barbie as invented personality. Barbie as a physical entity remains respectable. Barbie as an invented personality does not. Her transformation is the product of the popular culture that causes her to shape and respond to the societal standards. Therefore, the way in which to value the respectability of the Barbie doll, is to question the personal values and respectability of ourselves.

Gaze Into My Eyes

John Berger has famously stated that "Men act, women appear," yet over the developed understanding of this analysis, the statement: Men act, Barbie reappears, shall prevail. The examination of the Barbie image has been perceived as the abstraction of popular culture and societal ideals. These ideals were formulated for females by the desires of men, and the womanly appeal is determined by masculine surveillance. Therefore, the woman surrenders control as she is dominated by what Berger terms the "male gaze."

The "male gaze" is the objectification of women in mass culture. The female figure is to comply with the calculating stare of a man. As men in contemporary society witness and define the images of beauty, the paradigm of the Barbie doll is a welcomed addition. The women in society relinquish the central foundation of control found within their grasp, and their compliance to the male desires of perfection do not adhere to the standard of honesty designating the accused to "look them straight in the eye." Therefore, the delusion of honesty within women, and the imagery of the Barbie doll, continue to reflect this influenced acceptance.

Barbie does not follow this description of averting the male gaze, however she does maintain the explication of male desires. At the time of the Barbie doll's creation in 1959 until the year 1971, Barbie's eyes had been cast down and to one side— the deflected, submissive gaze that characterized the female form in artistic representations. As the culture transformed, it discovered that a woman could be both sexual and unashamed, therefore, the incarnation of Barbie was molded to the form that she was permitted to have the ideal physical dynamism, and look straight ahead (Lord 12).

In his work <u>Ways of Seeing</u>, Berger intricately examines the featured glance of a woman fitting the depiction of the "surveyed" or the "observed." She meets the glare of the male gaze, as does the Barbie doll, but affirms the role of active/male, passive/female. In addition, not only men, but due to the consenting critique of the male perception, women objectify women, and they begin by objectifying themselves. The position of the surveyor versus the surveyed projects illusion onto the female figure, which is styled accordingly. Womanly appearance is coded for strong visual and sexual impact, so it can be determined that the female connotes "to-be-looked-at-ness"(Lord 103). Following the patterned representation, Barbie formed as a semblance of the sexual evolution within women in popular culture in 1971, and Berger concurred, presenting his mastered theory in her shadow shortly one year later.

Dream Girls

She appeared at a time when the term "teenager" was a new and rather racy one. It was strongly questionable as to whether the American public would be ready for a doll with a womanly figure, but with a fresh face and fashions to fit every fantasy, women were identifying with the Barbie doll at a hastened pace.

Barbie was the representation of an alternative— a life before marriage, without disregarding the common values that complimented this lifestyle. She transformed the traditional behaviors of the sixties, and made them appear strikingly glamorous. However, these roles would soon change, and Mattel would need to assure that the evolution of the Barbie doll was continued and maintained, and the corporation has successfully achieved this standard. The Barbie doll has consistently been formed as a paradigm of the times, and women's ability to identify with her image has been captivating.

Mattel has even made it possible for women of different ethic backgrounds and cultures to find an individual identity with the Barbie doll. To exhibit her acceptance and modernity, the corporation has introduced an abundance of ethnic dolls within the Barbie line, as well as "Share a Smile Becky" to the marketplace. This doll was formed with a physical disability, yet it is uncertain as to why Becky and not Barbie was represented as having the impairment. Is Mattel as "socially aware" and sensitive as our culture had envisioned?

Outraged by the perceived behavior of the Barbie doll, feminists fiercely argued that Barbie's dream house was not even wheel chair accessible. In addition, it was found to be impossible that Barbie, who was defined by some as a "racist and sexist construction of a non-living being," could find a safe haven on the "Women's History Month" poster (Chamberlain 61). However, there she stood poised and proud because at least one female found her to be an accurate symbol of womanhood. This displaced anger falls heavily on the opposing side of those filled to the depths of admiration, yet the creation of that anger needs to also create a reminiscence within ourselves that the Barbie doll is a representation of an image. It is an image that Western culture and society have devised— not Barbie, and it strikes as an unfair fight if the doll in question is simply incapable of defending herself.

Barbie will continually hold the position of an object of feminist debate. From establishing the Barbie Liberation Organization, to naming her "one of the most excellent feminist teaching tools of all if seen as an institution," the members of the feminist movement both adore and criticize this icon. The center of the disagreement thrives and flourishes outward because Barbie was made by women for women. She was molded in the image and likeness of females, however she can seem to become the epitome of disillusion. Some feminists, who have even claimed to aggressively support the movement, also find appreciation for the Barbie doll. This small group feels that Barbie offers more to women than only pink and plastic.

The interpretations of the doll are purely individual, often being described as "useless beauty" or "empty glamour," however Barbie is a mere reflection of the expectations of society. The contributing editor of *Barbie Bazaar* magazine stated that, "People today are taking Barbie and really making it a mannequin that they drape their own dreams on." As feminists strive to have their voice heard in a variance of tones, it is seemingly ironic that not even Barbie resounds the same tune with every presence. Mattel has made it a point to alter the voice of the doll with each commercial, video, and computer program so that one may never become accustomed to a certain identity, and will allow themselves the pleasures of the imagination, mentally hearing their own voice in the place of their treasured icon.

Currently, the image of "Real Dolls" are also recreating an identification to the images of beauty, domination, and mental fantasy. Designed as a form of life-size Barbie, but are not associated with the Barbie doll line or the Mattel corporation, the dolls are modeled entirely of silicone, are highly realistic, and are presented on the market complete with a $4000 retail price. The artist who sculpted this cultural image of perfection explains that it is impossible for the model to compete with a human companion, but it is plausible to use the doll as a way to fulfill a deep void within the male existence (Langston 1). Therefore, the "Real Dolls" are the tangible expression of what mass society and popular culture have requested, and further illustrates the reasons to explain the need within women to secure this glorified identity.

The image of the Barbie icon began four decades ago, and it is when the Barbie doll established the position that she is a representation of someone with whom women could strongly identify. Currently, the evolution of the Barbie doll has taken her to the height of analysis and inquiry. She reigns supreme as a victor of all things possible for women, and she falls to a tragic destruction as the unattainable ideal who promotes negativity and poor self-actualization. There appears to be an absence of balance for this image of identification, and the most recent development for the Barbie doll quickly reignites the inferno.

The Barbie doll is encountering a physical reconstruction. Headlines ardently exploded from the mass media into the popular culture in a fervent manner. The following examples stated: "Barbie Loses Her Glamorous Image," "The New Barbie: It's Swell," and "Toward Greater Physical Reality." Each printed article reflected the differentiating tone of the authors, both male and female, who seemingly slipped away from the realm of objectivity, and quickly divulged into an interpersonal perception. Although, whether their tone hailed a sense of sarcasm or an expression of relief, each adhered to the principle that it was a positive enhancement.

Barbie is said to represent an unrealistic standard of beauty for women and young girls, so Mattel is attempting to update her look, concentrating on facial changes such as less makeup, a closed mouth, straighter hair, and a finer nose. The new model will also include body changes such as a fuller waist, slimmer hips, and a smaller bust. She will be named "Really Rad Barbie," and by the conclusion of 1998, Mattel proposed that six of 24 versions will be replaced with the refreshed appearance. Each of the mentioned characteristics and featured enrichments will begin to set the focus of reality for the Barbie doll with greater precision.

Exploring the construction of actuality, the average American woman would need to increase two feet in height, add five inches to her chest dimensions, and diminish six inches from her waistline (Devlin 15).

The newfound physical change for the Barbie doll is intended to reflect the expectations of the culture. Barbie has enchanted us for many years, although perhaps now "the magic has gone out of the relationship and it is time for something new"(White 1). However, is it that Mattel is providing another version of the famed doll as an improved product and social revelation; or is it that the women in popular culture are actively searching for an identity that is somewhat more simplistic and acceptable to attain?

Barbie has served as an inspiration to women for many remarkable decades. Those who criticize this image and icon address the Barbie doll in a variety of compositions, yet it is those who choose to appreciate her and her beauty, who develop an intricate connection that may be discussed, but can be impossible to sever. Therefore, women of different ethic backgrounds, beliefs, values, and ages form a relationship and identification with Barbie on an individual plain. She is a representation of all that they deem as possible. She can ascend from their imagination, or she can awaken from their hearts. The presentation of the Barbie doll in the mass media or in the mass market will impact the perspectives of those who witness this icon, however the perceptions of the mass media and the mass market are simply reproductions of what the popular culture has already made aware.

Can women become Barbie and fulfill this need for identification? Some hold the belief that this is not possible stating that, "She holds the illusory promise of inclusion— you love her, identify with her, want to be like her, and you can't. It's a betrayal from the very heart of things" (Chamberlain 62). Others passionately feel that her image is obtainable, crucial, and instrumental in providing the societal recognition that they desire to achieve.

Reality Barbie

It commenced as the implementation of the Barbie doll in the poignancy of the imagination. "Barbie was more than a doll to me. She was a way of living: the Ideal Woman. When I played with her, I could make her do and be anything I wanted. Never before or since have I found such an ideal method of living vicariously through anyone or anything" (Jackson 1).

Her name is Cindy Jackson. Forty-two years of age and registered with the British Internal Revenue as the Bionic Woman, she has been consistently reconstructing her physical appearance into the iconic image of desire— a Barbie doll. The examination of the doll and her glamorous lifestyle was to Jackson a parallel symbol of womanhood, and the attraction persisted until her visualization was immersed into reality. Jackson acknowledges that she has been cultivating a barrier between herself and the outside world that she describes as "shallow" and "predictable." She proclaims that her acceptance into the popular culture and society will only be formulated when she has achieved the "right look" in its entirety. Therefore, Jackson is striving to become the representation of the defined characteristics of attractiveness.

The medical personnel who have assisted Jackson in her quest, state that her emulation of the Barbie doll is scarcely uncommon. The image of Barbie was designed to become the paradigm of a woman, and it is the interpretation of the majority's perception of a pleasing physical semblance. It comprises the definition of "attractive." Therefore, it is said that if you were to poll a group of individuals to compose their image of beauty, what would be uncovered is someone who closely matches the ideological description of Jackson. This is the reasoning behind Jackson's now popular perspective, that if her look ever fades, she will be forced to exile contemporary society.

It seems impossible and undesirable that women, many of whom are following the path of Jackson, could find a relation of themselves to the Barbie doll in this manner. However, as each caught a glimpse of their "unacceptable" reflection, they appeared viciously flawed and concluded that the only option for the culture was to treat them accordingly. Therefore, instead of facing this inner collapse, many women select the construction of an alternative — "a very intentional, specific design to evoke human responses. And it works" (Honan 2).

She feels that what she has accomplished is the ultimate feminist statement saying, "Not only is no man going to control my life and my finances, but nature is not going to dictate the life that I should have just because I missed out in the generic lottery" (Honan 5). This perspective resides on the basis of truth for Jackson, supporting the proclamation that feminism is compiled on the restoration of the balance of power. However, if her quest is for balance and equality, why is she aspiring to acquire a colossal domination over the male gender?

As she endures to influence and taunt men with her treasured beauty, she finds that with her success, many other women are mesmerized with the opportunity to also join in this venture for power. Since Jackson's introduction, she has inspired an anonymous entourage of "clones" who are scattered around the world. After 27 threatening surgical procedures, Jackson has said that there was a time when she was concerned about losing her touch of individuality with so many attempting to duplicate her look. Now however, Jackson feels flattery in place of concern, and for her, this newfound appearance has become a profitable enterprise.

Jackson has made two primary contributions to mass society and popular culture: her seemingly enticing image, and her marketable technique. The superficiality of her nature which she finds admissible to condemn about society, is simply a product of the culture, and embraces little value. She is a commodity of the media, the market, and the mind. The image of Cindy Jackson is a creation of many individual perspectives and symmetries of the ideal standard of beauty. Therefore, Jackson did not design her own destiny, and she is not in control of the auspicious domination that she

74

perceives. Rather, it was the cultural perception of the Mattel corporation, the evolution of the Barbie doll, the mastery of the medical community, and her tainted misconception that beauty is only skin deep.

Jackson is misguided in her quest for splendor and idealism, and to look and live like Barbie is not the creation of attainable reality. Jackson was correct in her original assumption that the traces of her individuality were quickly fading when others appeared as the reproduction of her ideology. How is it even plausible that she could attest to possessing an individual identity when she was the replicated image of a non-living cultural icon? In his text Ways of Seeing, Berger presents the conceptuality of the original and the copy. Jackson is the representation of a copy at the quintessential extreme.

The mass marketed image of perfection, as exemplified by the Barbie doll, is the limitation of values and the expansion of contrived interpretation. In the previous discussion concerning the representation of respectability surrounding the image of the Barbie doll, are the conclusions of that debate evidenced in Jackson? As she forms her lifestyle to fit the mold of the illusionary world of Barbie, Jackson neglects the promise that the Barbie doll is structured to parallel the values of the middle class. Instead, Jackson lives an elite life of elegance, and appears to have a lesser respect for her personal being, than for the fulfillment of "respectability" as perceived by those members of mass culture.

In addition, as brutally exploited women working in a dynamics factory in Thailand produce Barbie dolls for First World children, they explore the existence of Jackson painfully in their minds. "For them, it would be unbearable to live a life looking like Barbie" (Foek 2). Therefore, can Jackson and the Barbie doll fully compete in this culture of imagery and ideals with the absence of value; or do they thrive among a commercial environment that not only produced their identity, but has captivated their control and lays claim to the possession of their spirit?

Chapter Five
Discussion Part Two: Marketing Analysis

Built to Last

"New for '59, the Barbie doll: A shapely teenage fashion model! Retail price $3.00..."(Riddick 1). The announcement distinguished the invention and introduction of the Barbie doll. She was a sophisticated display of the female form, consistently clothed with grace and style, and made her commanding debut at the International American Toy Fair in New York City.

Initially, the Barbie doll was met with questionable concern, and it was concluded that her acceptance into the realm of popular culture would require additional creativity. Therefore, Ruth Handler again needed to explore the unique attachment females actively developed with paper dolls, and then make a precise comparison to the collective design of the Barbie doll. The discovery she obtained was that similar to the success of paper dolls possessing interchangeable outfits, a varied accompaniment of fashions for Barbie also needed to be featured. In addition, there was a strong importance to maintain and conform to strict detail. The delicate pieces such as a purse, shoes, and jewelry enhanced the likelihood of capturing and mesmerizing the imagination.

As with the critical initiation of any product into the mass market, the Barbie doll was also met with a flourish of advertising and marketing techniques. For example, Herbert J. Holland, sales and merchandising manager for the Mattel corporation, used a Viewmaster to allow consumers to insert small diskettes, enabling them to visually experience how each outfit created for

Barbie would appear on the doll. Mattel offered retail stores an assortment of dolls, costumes, and Viewmasters to market the new line and increase sales. Another tool used to present the doll to retail stores was a graphically designed catalog which pictured the extensive creation of dolls and fashions available. Lastly, pink lucite case were constructed to hold an average of sixteen dressed Barbie dolls that were mounted to counters of retail stores to display the line of Barbie fashions.

  Each of the marketing techniques observed at the onset of the doll's presentation to the public, overcame the initial apprehension and began a profitable journey. Therefore, armed with a team of significantly imaginative employees with an affluent entrepreneurial profile, the innovative flair of the Mattel corporation took Barbie to the height of toy achievement (Westenhouser 14,15).

  Barbie soon became a merchandiser's dream. Her image could be uncovered on an array of items, including hardcover books, trading cards, doll cases, lunchboxes, paper dolls, and coloring books (Fennick 21). However, the most superior method to calculate the transcendence of Mattel's marketing of the Barbie doll is strongly reflected in the number of members who were enrolled in the Barbie Fan Club shortly after her introduction. At this time, the membership exceeded 600,000 which made it second in membership only to the Girl Scouts of America (Westenhouser 15).

The early years of Barbie's orientation to the mass market were substantially prosperous, and they established her position in the hearts of the American public and have continued to adhere to that stature ever since. For nearly four decades, the Barbie doll has become an international icon of perfected imagery, style, and femininity. However, despite her original and enduring acceptance, she has undergone a gradual metamorphosis to reflect the constant change in the standards of beauty, fashion, and ideology of popular culture (Fennick 12).

It is the now the dawning of a new age. Barbie has vastly embraced the future, and is catapulting into the idealistic year of 1999. She has commanded universal appeal, but it is the job of the Mattel corporation to maintain her image, and reside with the ongoing challenge of keeping her young, fresh and exciting. The primary goal of the organization is to ensure that they are aware of what consumers desire for the doll before it is expressed. Due to this accomplishment, Barbie is by far Mattel's strongest enterprise.

In 1997, the brand generated a significant sum of $1.7 billion in sales, which was approximately 40% of total revenues of $4.5 billion (Morgenson 47). Barbie also acclaims 40 registered trademarks which have spawned over 100 isolated products not associated with Barbie dolls and immediate accessories within the line. She has masterfully subsumed the fashion doll market. In America, 260 million people are quickly becoming identified by the prevalent statistics that affiliate them with the Barbie doll. These statistics prove that 95 percent of young females are estimated to own eight dolls, and for the adult market, Barbie is pronounced as a profound stock option and powerful collector success. However, in the element of each of these astounding details, the highest conquest of the Mattel corporation is that: every second, two Barbie dolls are sold across the country— a widespread domination unlike any other (Berens 1).

Mainstream Marketing

There is a masterful integration of individuals, divisions, and departments that retain purposeful intervention in the Barbie doll's development as it moves from concept through production. The following is the descriptive categorization of the processes necessary for the invention and reinvention of the ideological illusions of the Barbie doll.

- *"Manufacturing*, to determine the viability of producing the doll on time.

- *Costing*, to determine how the company will financially fare on the doll.

- *Management and scheduling*, to calculate when the doll is needed for the market.

- *Chemical and Safety Laboratories*, to identify potential quality and health issues with the planned doll.

- *The Hair Department*, to work closely with the designer in creating an appropriate hair style for the doll, to be consistent with both the designer's vision and the various constraints set by costing, scheduling, and safety.

- *Face painting*, again to work closely with the designer to realize makeup that is consistent and complementary to the design.

- *Face sculpting*, to create a new head mold, or to select an existing head mold.

- *Engineers*, to provide input on technical aspects of the doll, such as computer chips for speaking, pliability for bending the dolls, etc.

- *Textiles*, for designing and then sourcing the fabrics for the dolls.

- *Production pattern making*, to design the pattern for the costume" (Sarasohn-Kahn 207, 208).

In addition to the above marketing and production features, the contemporary art medium of advertising is also notably relevant. Advertising has played a key role in the promotional campaign of the

Barbie doll since her cultural and product establishment in 1959. A primary approach was to use television advertising which was purchased during central spots on the "Mickey Mouse Club." Barbie ads have also been placed in the print media, with the integral focus on magazines. "Today ads for the Barbie doll have gone well beyond traditional television, and have evolved into thirty-minute infomercials and offers through electronic catalogs over on-line computer services, along with the proliferation of print catalogs" (Sarasohn-Kahn 218).

With each of these elements within the industry striving to secure corporate proficiency as well as cultural identification, it is clear as to why Barbie has currently become more than simply a toy. She is an identity within mass culture. Adult Barbie t-shirts, eating utensils, posters, doll clothes and accessories, and a multitude of other items are commercially available. It is even possible to acquire an animated Barbie aerobics video, and participate in an adult Barbie look-alike competition, which adds to the stream of profitability of an unrelated business endeavor (Norton 287). In addition, Mattel licences products under the name of "Barbie for Girls" which appears on such items as shoes sold at the Payless Shoe Source chain. The Mattel corporation also jointly operates 17 independent boutiques in the United States with toy retailer FAO Schwarz, as well as two in the Canadian arena with the Hudson Bay Company retail chain (Mason 1).

However, because Barbie is so easily identifiable, the marketing team at Mattel must take precautions as to how to use Barbie to market merchandise other than dolls, because they require the conservation of complete integrity for her as a brand (Riddick 5). This is the reasoning as to why the Mattel corporation does not subject the doll to the criticism and scrutiny that would occur if she was to appear in a television series or a movie role. Without the use of these mediums, Mattel can allow the storyline of the Barbie doll to be exceedingly open to the depths of the imagination.

The Barbie doll is also a case study in superior product development and marketing innovation. Each year, Mattel designs and produces approximately 90 different Barbies, including a variety of associated friends, family members, pets, and customized products for retailers. In addition, the Barbie doll has triumphed in becoming universally recognized. Her association with other popular mainstream brands have aided in this accomplishment. Examples of this include: Barbie's "Birthday Fun at McDonald's" set, a "Baywatch" rescue boat, the possession of a "Jeep," and her "Lee" jeans apparel.

By attaching her to culturally specific items and representations, Barbie strategically assimilates with them congruently. "People familiarize themselves with the images together, and as one increases or decreases in popularity, the other follows" (Riddick 4). Therefore, Barbie reigns as the most preferred doll within the mass market and popular culture, and she is a burgeoning industry in her own right. Among the nation's most recognized consumer icons, the Barbie doll ranks eminently with Coca-Cola, Levis and Campbell Soup (Mason 1).

Product of the Imagination

With the ample collection of Barbie dolls to choose from, Mattel has created a desire to own more than a single doll, by allowing each individual Barbie to offer a unique play situation. The corporation's core strategy has been segmentation in terms of price and play patterns. For example, the new "Gymnast Barbie" is the only doll within the line who has the ability to perform gymnast movements and routines (Mason 1). Other Barbie dolls at this time that are achieving national success, are the cheerleading Barbie dolls which provide support for 19 collegiate institutions, the presidential Barbie doll, and the controversial "Cool Shoppin' Barbie."

Barbie dolls have now been named as cheerleaders for a select number of colleges and universities. By allowing Barbie to wear their colors and promote their institution, the schools acquire more than the essence of high spirit. Each will receive an 8% royalty from the Mattel corporation with the purchase of every Barbie doll. Barbie is also dominating the culture and market to the theme of "We Girls Can Do Anything." However, this time Barbie is proving that "we" can even be boys. To celebrate the Fourth of July, the statuesque plaything is receiving a presidential makeover and becoming another acclaimed American icon— George Washington. It marks the first time that the Barbie doll has transformed and incarnated into a male figure (Baldwin 11).

Finally, in March of this year, Mattel announced that they had joined forces with the MasterCard corporation to present a shopping-themed Barbie doll to raise its image among children as young as three years of age. The doll comes fully equipped with a Barbie-sized MasterCard, and the credit enterprise has stated that, "this initiative was a great opportunity to promote brand awareness among collectors, parents, and future card holders. It empowers children to play out a realistic shopping adventure" (Choquette 6B).

Another primary impact that made the distinction between the Barbie doll of 1999 in comparison to the Barbie doll of 1959 was her presence in the work world. The nineties slogan "We Girls Can Do Anything" is again the resounding theme, serving as a representation of women across the country. Barbie was not simply presented as a stewardess, she was now the pilot, and she was pioneering the flight to the top of the ethereal workplace and sprinting over any mass-marketing obstacles that prevailed in her path. Therefore, "Barbie made the workplace, traditionally formidable for women, appear enchanting" (Riddick 1).

The Barbie doll is also recognized as a "global power brand." The Mattel corporation wanted to appeal to a wider market, so the face moldings were altered, and the development of an international line promptly took form. The dolls include an ethnic, cultural, and racial assortment which no longer rely on a separate personality within the Barbie line. Mattel did not need to dichotomize the doll's personalities; they could evolve into the same crafted image with varying skin tones. These changes reflected the multicultural direction of the country, and the increasing sales of these dolls proved Americans were accepting the equality of all races and nationalities (Riddick 1).

Today the Barbie doll is sold in 144 countries, and the extreme level of penetration in that market has yet to be achieved. Therefore, the growth potential of Barbie worldwide is beyond that of the United States (Mason 1). Barbie has transcended all socioeconomic boundaries permitting even children in the poorest countries to own her. "The reality is in the reproduction. Most human icons are possessed only through film or audiotape; the 'original' forever eludes ownership. Barbie, however, is meant to be owned not by a few, but by everyone (Lord 73). Therefore, as Berger would describe, Barbie is the ultimate piece of mass art.

Due to the global recognition of the Barbie doll, the differentiating cultural traditions and perceptions need to also be considered with the introduction of a innovative product. An example of this discord is witnessed in the country of Iran. Islamic headliners have deemed Barbie dolls as "satanic" in an attempt to dissuade consumers from making individual purchases. The Islamic leaders say that "the unwholesome flexibility of these dolls, their destructive beauty, and their semi-nudity have an effect on the minds and morality of young children" (Hayes 1). However, buyers continue to find an adoration for the doll, and despite a severe economic crisis, Barbies are selling for exorbitant prices of 300,000 rials ($80 dollars) to a million rials ($250 dollars). "In other words, they are selling between one and three times the average monthly wage" (Hayes 1).

On the American horizon, the most recent phenomenon of the Barbie doll is her appearance and emergence into the marketing realm of the computer era. "Talk With Me Barbie" made its successful debut in the summer of 1997, and was designed to perform as the imitation of an authentic person. For the first time, buyers would be able to program Barbie with an individual personality by connecting the doll and her computer to the family PC. "Talk With Me Barbie" is packaged with a Windows 95 compatible CD-Rom, batteries, and in her pink accessories tote: a notebook computer, cassette player, and a cellular phone are discovered, again facilitating the essence of the imagination (Howells 1).

In addition to this modernization within the breadth of technological advancement, Mattel also offers "Barbie Print and Play" developed to create your own Barbie stationery and stickers, and "Barbie Story Maker" which fosters your capacity to direct her in a short film complete with sound and special effects. To maintain the beauty and fashion standards, "Barbie Fashion Designer" which allows the consumer to design and print out tangible costumes for the doll, as well as "Barbie Magic Hair Styler" which enables the buyer to interact with the doll by cutting and shaping her hair, are also presently available (Howells 2).

More Than a Fashion Statement

"The doll sells the clothes, and the clothes sell the doll" (Riddick 1). This dynamic thought has continued to hail as the truism of the Mattel corporation since the time of the familiarization with the Barbie doll. In 1959, Handler aspired to devise a stunning wardrobe from which each female child could choose an outfit, and conceive her own personality for Barbie. Therefore, Handler desired to develop fashions that would coordinate with the societal aspirations and expectations of the popular culture (Riddick 2).

To remain constant with the marketing axiom that prevailed among Mattel members, clothes that could only be described as "meticulous and eye-catching" were assembled to the Barbie wardrobe. The featured fashions of this product evolve from year to year, and they reflect the influential styles of the period. Therefore, the detail detected with a mere glance at the Barbie doll was far from accidental for the Mattel corporation. They consistently hold the determination to produce quality in the doll line and in the fashion structure (Westenhouser 28, 29).

Taking a cultural stance in the application of Barbie fashion, "fans of conspiracy theories will be disappointed to learn that Barbie's proportions were not the result of some misogynistic plot. They were dictated by the mechanics of clothing construction" (Lord 2). The fabrics that Barbie displays are scaled accordingly to the human form, even though she is one-sixth the size of a person. Her initial designer delicately informed that her middle had to be disproportionately narrow to look proportional in clothing (Lord 2). A factual explanation that may prove surprising is in regard to the reformation of the more "realistically" designed Barbie recently preparing to be introduced.

Although feminists have long protested that the Barbie form was promoting an unattainable image for females, Mattel announced that they are sensitive to this issue, however the newly developed Barbie doll is purely a reflection of changing fashionable ages. The new figure will allow Barbie to slip into current teen designs, such as hip-hugging jeans (Sapsted 1). Therefore, the marketing opportunity will again arise to sell the transformed doll, as well as her contemporary line of coordinating fashions.

In the global arena, an independent element of Barbie fashion and style is arising. The Japanese fashion company, Itochu Fashion System Co. plans to produce a substantial monetary sum of adult-size Barbie handbags, earrings, pajamas, undergarments and dresses. Mattel will lease its name and logo to the Japanese corporation for the development of a Barbie inspired adult line, designed to fit women 15 to 25 years of age. The Barbie doll is an ominous success in Japan- "a nation passionate for fads, brand names, and fashion trends" (Ferguson 1). When asked for the reasoning behind their fascination with the petite and lively blonde ideal, a representative simply replied, "We are looking to tap into the Barbie lifestyle, the Barbie way of life" (Ferguson 1).

The year 1998 was also the time for Mattel to contrive an effective response to collectors internationally. Producing a substantial line of adult Barbie additions, several aspects were improved. The quality of the dolls: better face molds, makeup, clothing, accessories, and details; the number of dolls: more limited, more exclusive distribution; and the lower overall price points, were each enhanced (Sarasohn-Kahn 101). To demonstrate the abundance and interest within collectors, the "Barbie Bazaar" magazine is an explicit example.

This publication, targeted to the predominant audience of adult females, has a readership of over 20,000 twice a month. Detailed in this periodical, are the line of collector dolls, highlighting popular designers such as Mackie, Dior and Lauren. This assembly of professionals produce exquisite fashions for the Barbie doll which has acclaimed elegance and glamour for this image, this icon, and this ideal.

Manufacturing Respect

Two definitive time periods in history have been analytically represented in this thesis: 1959 and 1999. The marketing trends prevalent during each of these strategic years were individual entities, yet they are the foundational elements of achievement for the Barbie doll who continues to evolve. Throughout her existence, the Barbie doll has fostered creativity, product development and mass sales. However, has the company that produced this icon, manufactured the intangible?

Has the Mattel corporation presented to the mass market a doll of value, honor and respectability that she alone can exclusively uphold and protect?

It was concluded in Part One that the cultural identity of Barbie as associated with the issue of respectability, was a solid reflection of the societal dominion. The attachment or absence of value was placed onto the Barbie doll by her individual beholder. It was the depiction of the cultural consensus as to how "respectability" needed to be defined when held within the context of a precise image. Therefore, the possessor of the doll would recognize that description and formulate a unique construction of respect. However, in the limitation of the marketing element, the respectability of the image is derived solely in the hands of her maker.

The Mattel corporation has fiercely claimed to perpetuate the standards of respectability for the Barbie doll since the time of her creation. It was said that she was not built on beauty, rather she was built on the premise of character, and has maintained that honor for nearly forty years. From a marketing perspective, the recognition of this quality found within the Barbie doll is reproduced in her array of tasteful occupations, fashions and designs. She has been granted a life that is full of illusionary promise and success, and it is the appearance of a wholesome American girl surrounded by other "respectable" figures.

Taking each of these facets into consideration, the actual realization of respectability within the marketplace falls to the perception of the industry. As a product phenomenon, the Barbie doll has surpassed and capitalized on an image, and the Mattel corporation has formed her into a legend of insurmountable capacity. No other fashion doll has risen to the eminence of toy profitability, recognition, and identification as the Barbie doll has consistently upheld and maintained. It is necessary to disregard both the cultural implications of value and the reflection of Mattel-induced "respectability." Therefore, the emphatic prosperity of the Barbie doll continues to substantiate a conscious claim: To place a value on respect within any context or denomination, is not that which has been manufactured, but that which has been earned.

Chapter Six
Conclusion

"The Image of Us All"

She is the image of our creation, the image of our fantasy, and the image of our future. Therefore, the analysis of the Barbie doll does not seem to warrant an intentional conclusion. Her initiation into the mass media and mass culture, as well as her current practices and representations have been monumentally defined throughout the scope of this thesis. However, the wealth of knowledge to be discovered about the Barbie doll does not lie within these pages of analytical thought, rather it rests within the shadow of the Barbie figure as perceived by the human mind.

It is clearly evident that the cultural and corporate identification with the Barbie doll prevails on an adult level of female acceptance. It was observed how Barbie takes precedence within the expectations of society as a pop cultural icon. The statistics have been discovered, and the perspectives have been both addressed and explored. However, the desire to assimilate into the illusionary lifestyle of the Barbie doll still remains a dominant mystery.

As one journeys through the forum of the public sphere, and experiences firsthand the dedication and admiration for a constructed image, one begins to wonder if the appreciation of the Barbie doll initiates from within. As Barbie is considered the realization of an actual image, is there an acknowledgment present to the acceptance or denial of a doll formed as a product of another's imagination? The answer to this question is unclear, however, Barbie has matured slowly and has

Association w/ doll means allowing a company to build your identity.

allowed Mattel to also adhere to a coherent focus of the doll's identity. Additionally, the corporation has projected the imagery of the Barbie doll passionately onto the minds and hearts of the significantly impressionable public.

Mattel's marketing and advertising techniques have centered on these cultural patterns. Within the inner depths of Mattel, the corporation has followed current fashions and fads, and has chosen only those that will maintain Barbie's grace on top of the glorified pedestal on which America has placed her. "They have transformed controversial and potentially threatening issues into opportunities, and have kept Barbie as the adaptable yet stable emblem of the popular culture" (Riddick 1).

Shattering the Mold

This thesis has also examined the premier standards of beauty, idealism and femininity which were controlled as the foundations of achievement. Women lost sight of their value, and concurred with the male understanding of gender distinction. Some women found the rekindling of a memory, some discovered a model of perfection for which they could aspire, and some uncovered an image of destruction and unfair extremes that was virtually impossible to obtain. However, the common element within the determination of each of these women is that when they began their search to acquire a reminiscence, an ideal, or a delusion, what each of them found was a Barbie doll.

They ascertained the same image, but without identical meaning. The same doll in the same form, appears as the representation of something vastly different, and this is the resolution of where the connection between the cultural and marketing perspective becomes evident. The makers of the Barbie doll present an image that they desire to be accepted, and the culture has affirmed this certification for several decades.

The interpretation of an image by consumers and members of mass society and popular culture is what positions a paradigm similar to the Barbie doll, as unique to other iconic images. Unlike past recognizable icons who begin as a human identity and then capitalize on the marketplace with the vision of profitability, the Barbie doll evolved from the constraints of a manufactured form, and transcended into more than a physical object— she adhered to the practice of an invented personality.

The respectability of this ideal image was also examined throughout both the cultural and marketing phases. The discovery unveiled was that the "respectable" characteristics of value conceived within the domain of the Barbie doll, were strictly the formations of respect cast upon her and comprehended throughout the years of her existence. Again, it is the beholder of the Barbie doll who distinguishes the limitations of respect that this icon can envelop and exude.

In conclusion, the Barbie doll has remained an intricate piece of the cultural puzzle that flourishes and evolves with the unyielding commencement of time. She has been lavishly praised, and she has been fiercely criticized. However, the cultivation of emotion expressed as a society is the effect of both the development of her physical being, as well as her invented personality. Further, this impact underscores yet another pattern in the unrestricted element of the Barbie doll.

Individuals project fear and inequalities onto her; or they create an illumination in the essence of adoration. However, when one talks at length about the representations of the Barbie doll, one usually comes to conclude that they learn more about the ideologies and perceptions of the speaker than had ever been intended (Lord 298). Therefore, as the image has been reflected into the cultural mirror glaring into our conceptualized view, we find that to adore or criticize an icon such as the Barbie doll, seems to say a lot less about the imagery of this "ideal," and much more about the concealed illusions of ourselves.

Chapter Seven
Bibliography

Works Cited

Aqua. <u>Barbie Girl</u>. Compact Disc. Johnny Jam, Delgado, S. Rasted and C. Norreen. MCA Records, Universal City, 1997.

Baldwin, Kristen. "Dragging the Line." <u>Entertainment Weekly</u> n 387, 11 July 1997: 11.

Berens, Jessica. "The Barbie Army." <u>Electronic Telegraph</u> Issue 940 [Online] Available http://www.telegraph.co.uk/home.html, Dec. 20, 1997: 1-5.

Berger, John. <u>Ways of Seeing</u>. London: Penguin Books, 1977.

Borger, Gloria. "Barbie's Newest Values." <u>U.S. News and World Report</u> 123, n21, 1 Dec. 1997: 40-41.

Boxer, Sarah. "Photography Review: Beauty, in a Variety of Guises." <u>New York Times</u> 2 Sept. 1997: 1-2.

Brownmiller, Susan. <u>Femininity</u>. New York: Linden, 1984.

Chamberlain, Kathy. "Idollatry." <u>Tikkun</u> 10, n2 Mar.-Apr. 1995: 57-63.

Choquette, Kara K. "Not All Approve of Barbie's MasterCard." <u>USA Today</u> 30 Mar. 1998: 6B.

Cook, Diane. "Mattel's Garage." <u>Time Inc.</u> June 1996: 1.

Coward, Rosalind. <u>Female Desires: How They are Sought, Bought and Packaged</u>. New York: Grove Weidenfeld, 1985.

Crawford, Lisa. "Mattel Files Suit Against Danish Band Aqua." <u>Reuters/Variety</u> 12 Sept. 1997: 1.

Curry, Ramona. Too Much of a Good Thing: Mae West as Cultural Icon. Minneapolis: University of Minnesota, 1996.

Devlin, Colleen. "No Real-Life Barbie or Kens." Industry Week 245, n9, 6 May 1996: 15-16.

Dooley, Dennis and Gary Engle. Superman at Fifty: The Persistence of a Legend. Indianapolis: Macmillan Publishing Co., 1987.

Dyer, Richard. Stars. London: BFI, 1979.

Fennick, Janine. The Collectable Barbie Doll: An Illustrated Guide to Her Dreamy World. Philadelphia: Courage Books, 1996.

Ferguson, P.H. "Japanese Women Soon Can Get All Dolled Up Just Like Barbie." Source News and Reports. 17 Dec. 1996: 1-2.

Fiske, John. "Popular Culture." Understanding Popular Culture. New York: Routledge, 1989: 2-12.

---. "Commodities and Culture." Understanding Popular Culture. New York: Routledge, 1989: 23-47.

Foek, Anton. "Sweatshop Barbie: Dynamics Factory in Thailand." The Humanitarist Jan.-Feb. 1997: 1-2.

Freedman, Rita. Beauty Bound. New York: Lexington Books, 1986.

Groves, David. "A Doll's Life." Los Angeles Times 15 Dec. 1994, home ed.: 8+.

Harris, David. "Plastic Surgery Guru Inspires An Army of Clones." The Daily Telegraph June 1997: 1-3.

Hayes, Jessica. "Barbie Dolls 'Satanic'." Electronic Telegraph Issue 378 [Online] Available http://www.telegraph.co.uk/home.html, May 7, 1996: 1.

Honan, Corinna. "How Cindy Got Her Revenge On Men." Electronic Telegraph Issue 757 [Online] Available http://www.telegraph.co.uk/home.html, June 21,1997:1-6.

Howells, Jan. "There's Life in the Old Doll Yet." Electronic Telegraph Issue 697 [Online] Available http://www.telegraph.co.uk/home.html, Apr. 22, 1997: 1-3.

Hughes, Jane, and N'Gai Croal. "Lara Croft, the Bit Girl: How a Game Star Became a '90s Icon." Newsweek 130, n19, 10 Nov. 1997: 82-84.

Jackson, Cindy. "And Then I Created Another Cindy: Cindy Jackson Describes How She 'Cloned' Herself." Electronic Telegraph Issue 757 [Online] Available http://www.telegraph.co.uk/home.html, June 21, 1997: 1-3.

---. "Living Vicariously Through Barbie." [Online] Available http://ziris.syr.edu/path/public_html/barbie/main.html, May 2, 1995: 1.

Langston, James. "American Men Find True Love With a Real Doll." Electronic Telegraph Issue 849 [Online] Available http://www.telegraph.co.uk/home.html, Sept. 21, 1997: 1-2.

Lehrman, Karen. The Lipstick Proviso: Women, Sex & Power in the Real World. New York: Anchor Books, 1997.

Lord, M.G. Forever Barbie: The Unauthorized Biography of a Real Doll. New York: Avon Books, 1995.

Mason, Tom. "What Makes Barbie a Girl's Favorite Doll?" Investors Business Daily: Executive Update 12 Apr. 1995: 1-2.

Mattel Inc. Original Barbie Doll Theme. [Online] Available http://www.barbie.com, April 5, 1998.

---. "Welcome to Barbie.com: Official Barbie Doll Web Site." [Online] Available http://www.barbie.com, Jan. 3, 1998: 1-10.

McKenzie, Jean. "Barbie Gets a Whole New Look." [Online] Available http://www.barbie.com, 1998: 1.

Morgenson, Gretchen. "Saturation Barbie?" Forbes Magazine 160, n9, 20 Oct.1997: 46-47.

Norton, Kevin I., and Steven Dank; Timothy S. Olds; and Scott Olive. "Ken and Barbie at Life Size." Sex Roles: A Journal of Research 34, n3-4 Feb. 1996: 287-95.

Piercy, Marge. "Barbie Doll." [Online] Available http://www.capecod.net/~tmpiercy/ April 5, 1998: 1.

Priest, Susanna Hornig. <u>Doing Media Research: An Introduction</u>. London: Sage, 1996.

Quan, Tracy. "Understanding Barbie-Phobia." [Online] Available http://desires.com/1.2/words/docs/barbie1.html, Sept. 2, 1995: 1-2.

Riddick, Kristin. "Barbie: The Image of Us All." [Online] Available http://xroads.virgina.edu/~class/barbie/barb.html, Jan. 3, 1998: 1-18.

Robertson, Pamela. "Too Much of a Good Thing: Mae West as Cultural Icon." <u>Film Quarterly</u> 51, n1 Fall 1997: 61-63.

Rosaldo, Michelle Zimbalist. <u>Women, Culture, and Society</u>. New York: Stanford UP, 1974.

Sapsted, David. "Barbie, 38, Loses Her Glamorous 80's Image." <u>Electronic Telegraph</u> Issue 908 [Online] Available http://www.telegraph.co.uk/home.html, Nov. 18, 1997: 1-2.

Sarasohn-Kahn, Jane. <u>Contemporary Barbie: Barbie Dolls 1980 and Beyond</u>. Norfolk: Antique Trader Books, 1997.

Schneider, Cy. "Origin of Barbie." <u>Children's Television Script</u> (1987): 1-2.

Settle Robert, and Pamela Alreck. <u>Why They Buy, American Consumers Inside and Out</u>. New York: John Wiley and Sons Inc., 1989.

Stevenson, Nick. <u>Understanding Media Cultures: Social Theory and Mass Communications</u>. London: Sage, 1995.

Westenhouser, Kitturah. The Story of Barbie. Paducah,
    KY: Collector Books, 1994.
White, Michael. "Mattel Plans Barbie With Less
    Bosom, More Waist." Charlotte Observer 17
    Nov.
    1997: 1-2.
Williamson, Judith. Consuming Passions: The
    Dynamics of Popular Culture. London: Marion
    Boyars, 1995.
Wolf, Naomi. The Beauty Myth: How Images of Beauty
    Are Used Against Women. New York: Anchor
    Books, 1992.

Works Consulted

"All Dolled Up." The Economist 330, n7849, 5 Feb.
    1994: 66-67.

Anderson, Abby. "Diva of Dolls." MPLS-St. Paul
    Magazine 23, n1 (1995): 21-22.

Aqua. Barbie Girl. Compact Disc. Johnny Jam,
    Delgado, S. Rasted and C. Norreen. MCA
    Records, Universal City, 1997.

Ashabraner, Joan, and Sibyl DeWein. The Collectors
    Encyclopedia of Barbie Dolls and Collectibles.
    Paducah, KY: Collector Books, 1984.

Augustyniak, Michael J. The Barbie Doll Boom:
    Identification and Values. Paducah, KY:
    Collector Books, 1996.

---.   Identification and Values. Paducah, KY:
    Collector Books, 1997.

Bager, Peter. "Barbie Art." [Online] Available
    http:bigmouth.pathfinder.com/@@A2n0qeAAQJ
    2o/altculture/aentries/b/
    barbieexart.html, April 14, 1998: 1-2.

Baldwin, Kristen. "Dragging the Line." Entertainment
    Weekly n 387, 11 July 1997: 11.

Bannon, Lisa. "Top-Heavy Barbie is Getting Body
    Work at Hands of Mattel." Wall   Street Journal
    [New York] vol. ccxxx, n98, 17 Nov. 1997: A1+.

"Barbie's Bad Hair Day Has Collectors Seeing Pink."
    Time 149, n21, 26 May 1997: 62.

Barbie Bazaar. "The Barbie Doll Collector's
    Magazine." 10, Issue 3, Apr. 1998.

"Barbie's New Look: Digital." Time For Kids 2, n12, 13 Dec. 1996: 8-9.

"Barbie's New Software Career." Investor's Business Daily: Computers and Technology Feb. 1996: 1.

Barne, Kitty. Barbie. Boston: Little, Brown, 1969.

Benko, Laura B. "Barbie Chief Jean McKenzie Drives the Doll Market By Thinking, Playing Like a Kid." Investor's Business Daily- Leaders and Success. 25 Aug. 1997: 1-2.

Berens, Jessica. "The Barbie Army." Electronic Telegraph Issue 940 [Online] Available http://www.telegraph.co.uk/home.html, Dec. 20, 1997: 1-5.

Berger, John. Ways of Seeing. London: Penguin Books, 1977.

Blitman, Joe. Barbie and Her Mod, Mod, Mod World of Fashion 1967-1972. Grantsville, MD: Hobby House, 1996.

Boccella, Kathy. "New Barbie Will Have a Body More Like a Teen's." Philadelphia Inquirer. 18 Nov. 1997: 1-3.

Borger, Gloria. "Barbie's Newest Values." U.S. News and World Report 123, n21, 1 Dec. 1997: 40-41.

Boxer, Sarah. "Photography Review: Beauty, in a Variety of Guises." New York Times 2 Sept. 1997: 1-2.

Boy, Billy. Barbie: Her Life and Times and the New Theater of Fashion. New York: Crown, 1992.

Brown, Bob. "Becoming Barbie." 20/20. 28 June 1996.

---. "Barbie's Revenge: Woman Who Transformed Herself to Look Like Barbie." 20/20. 5 Jan 1998.

Brownmiller, Susan. Femininity. New York: Linden, 1984.

Brunner, Rob. "Plastic Surgin'." Entertainment Weekly n.393-94, 22 Aug. 1997: 14.

Cawley, Marianne. "Too Much of a Good Thing: Mae West as Cultural Icon." Library Journal. Baltimore: Epoch Pratt Free Library, 1996.

Chamberlain, Kathy. "Idollatry." Tikkun 10, n2 Mar.-Apr. 1995: 57-63.

Choquette, Kara K. "Not All Approve of Barbie's MasterCard." USA Today 30 Mar.1998: 6B.

Codrington, Andrea. "Dolls Are Exerting an Uncanny Power on Pop Culture." New York Times 147, n324, col.5, 20 Nov. 1997: F2.

Collinridge, Vanessa. "Sorry Guys, This Might Hurt a Bit." Electronic Telegraph Issue 816 [Online] Available http://www.telegraph.co.uk/home.html, Aug. 19, 1997: 1-2.

Cook, Diane. "Mattel's Garage." Time Inc. June 1996: 1.

Coward, Rosalind. Female Desires: How They are Sought, Bought and Packaged. New York: Grove Weidenfeld, 1985.

Crawford, Lisa. "Mattel Files Suit Against Danish Band Aqua." Reuters/Variety 12 Sept. 1997: 1.

Cross, Gary. Kids Stuff: Toys and the Changing Worlds of American Childhood. Cambridge, MA: Harvard UP, 1997.

Curnow, Kathy. "Prestige and the Gentleman: Benin's Ideal Man: How Men Look: On the Masculine Ideal and the Body Beautiful." Art Journal 56, n2 (1997): 75-82.

Curry, Ramona. Too Much of a Good Thing: Mae West as Cultural Icon. Minneapolis: University of Minnesota, 1996.

Davidson, Mark. Barbie Doll Structure and Furniture (Babbie). Grantsville, MD: Hobby House, 1997.

DeRosa, Robin. "Liberation of Barbie." USA Today 5 Jan. 1998: A2.

Deutsch, Stephanie. Barbie the First 30 Years 1959 Through 1989: An Identification and Value Guide. Paducah, KY: Collector Books, 1995.

Devlin, Colleen. "No Real-Life Barbie or Kens." Industry Week 245, n9, 6 May 1996: 15-16.

Dickey, Lisa. "Barbie to Russia With Love." [Online] Available http://www.friends-partners.org/oldfriends/spbweb/sppress/94/barbie.html, Feb. 15, 1998.

Dooley, Dennis and Gary Engle. Superman at Fifty: The Persistence of a Legend. Indianapolis: Macmillan Publishing Co., 1987.

Dowd, Maureen. "Barbie Pulls Teeth." New York Times 146, col.5, 6 Aug. 1997:A15+.

Dyer, Richard. Stars. London: BFI, 1979.

Eames, Sarah Sink. Barbie Fashion: 1959-1967 Vol.1. Paducah, KY: Collector Books, 1990.

---. Barbie Doll Fashion: 1968-1974 Vol. 2. Paducah, KY: Collector Books, 1997.

---. Barbie Rarities: The Dolls the Costumes Miscellany. Grantsville, MD. Hobby House, 1994.

Ebersole, Lucinda, and Richard Peabody. Mondo Barbie: An Anthology of Fiction and Poetry. New York: St. Martin's, 1993.

Eisner, Jane R. "A New 'Joy' and a New Barbie! Hip Hip Hooray!" Philadelphia Inquirer 23 Nov. 1997: E7.

Faraone, Jim. Fashion Doll Makeovers: Learn from the Artists. Grantsville, MD: Hobby House, 1996.

Fennick, Janine. The Collectable Barbie Doll: An Illustrated Guide to Her Dreamy World. Philadelphia: Courage Books, 1996.

Ferguson, P.H. "Japanese Women Soon Can Get All Dolled Up Just Like Barbie." Source News and Reports. 17 Dec. 1996: 1-2.

Fiske, John. "Popular Culture." Understanding Popular Culture. New York: Routledge, 1989: 2-12.

---. "Commodities and Culture." Understanding Popular Culture. New York: Routledge, 1989: 23-47.

Foek, Anton. "Sweatshop Barbie: Dynamics Factory in Thailand." The Humanitarist Jan.-Feb. 1997: 1-2.

Frease, Amy. "All About Barbie!" [Online] Available http://ziris.syr.edu/path/public_html/barbie/art.html, Apr. 22, 1997:1-3.

Freedman, Rita. Beauty Bound. New York: Lexington Books, 1986.

Grant, John. Encyclopedia of Walt Disney's Animated Characters. New York: Hyprion, 1993.

Groves, David. "A Doll's Life." Los Angeles Times 15 Dec. 1994, home ed.: 8+.

Hagen, Jessica. "Barbie FAQ." [Online] Available http://www.visi.com/~jessica/index.html, Mar. 1, 1998: 1-6.

Hall, Stuart. Questions of Cultural Identity. London: Sage, 1996.

Handler, Ruth and Jacqueline Shannon. Dream Doll. California: Longmeadow Press, 1997.

Harris, David. "Plastic Surgery Guru Inspires An Army of Clones." The Daily Telegraph June 1997: 1-3.

Hayes, Isobel. "Why I Became a 'Double'." Electronic Telegraph Issue 757 [Online] Available http://www.telegraph.co.uk/home.html, June 21, 1997: 1-3.

Hayes, Jack. "Burying Barbie." MPLS-St. Paul's Magazine 24, n6 June 1996: 18-20.

Hayes, Jessica. "Barbie Dolls 'Satanic'." Electronic Telegraph Issue 378 [Online] Available http://www.telegraph.co.uk/home.html, May 7, 1996: 1.

Holland, Kelley. "'Gee, Ken, Look At All This Bread!'" Business Week n3551, 3 Nov. 1997: 50.

Honan, Corinna. "How Cindy Got Her Revenge On Men." Electronic Telegraph Issue 757 [Online] Available http://www.telegraph.co.uk/home.html, June 21,1997: 1-6.

Howard, Joseph. "The New Barbie It's Swell." Press of
Atlantic City 24 Nov. 1997: 1-2.

Howells, Jan. "There's Life in the Old Doll Yet."
Electronic Telegraph Issue 697 [Online]
Available
http://www.telegraph.co.uk/home.html, Apr. 22,
1997: 1-3.

Hughes, Jane, and N'Gai Croal. "Lara Croft, the Bit
Girl: How a Game Star Became a '90s Icon."
Newsweek 130, n19, 10 Nov. 1997: 82-84.

Irwin, Victoria Cebalo. "Hello Dolly!" Parenting 10,
n10 Dec.-Jan. 1996: 140-47.

Jackson, Cindy. "And Then I Created Another Cindy:
Cindy Jackson Describes How She 'Cloned'
Herself." Electronic Telegraph Issue 757
[Online] Available
http://www.telegraph.co.uk/home.html, June 21,
1997: 1-3.

---. "Living Vicariously Through Barbie." [Online]
Available
http://ziris.syr.edu/path/public_html/barbie/main.
html, May 2, 1995: 1.

Jacobs, A.J., and Jessica Shaw. "Legend of the Doll."
Entertainment Weekly n263-64
24 Feb. 1995: 16-17.

Jacobs, Laura. Barbie in Fashion (Tiny Folio Series).
New York: Abbeville, 1997.

---.   Barbie: What a Doll! New York: Abbeville, 1994.

Johnson, Christopher. "Toward Greater Physical Reality." Alibi News 26 Nov-Dec. 1997: 2.

Kendrick, Sheryl. "Just Me and My Barbie." [Online] Available http://pascal.acm.org/~sheryl/barbie.html, Mar. 16, 1998: 1.

Kile, Crystal. "Barbie and Me." [Online] Available http://ernie.bgsu.edu/~ckile/barbie.html, Feb. 24, 1998: 1-4.

Langston, James. "American Men Find True Love With a Real Doll." Electronic Telegraph Issue 849 [Online] Available http://www.telegraph.co.uk/home.html, Sept. 21, 1997: 1-2.

Lehrman, Karen. The Lipstick Proviso: Women, Sex & Power in the Real World. New York: Anchor Books, 1997.

Lescher, Vicky. "Barbie Trivia." [Online] Available http://www.sn:.com.tr/~visky/barbie/btrivia.html, Apr. 15, 1997: 1-2.

Lewin, Tamar. "Flatter, Smarter and Socially Sensitive." New York Times 147, col.3 29 Nov. 1997: A15+.

Lieberman, Rhonda. "Goys and Dolls." Artforum 33, n8 Apr. 1995: 21-23.

Lindlof, Thomas R. Qualitative Communication Research Methods. London: Sage, 1995.

Lord, M.G. Forever Barbie: The Unauthorized Biography of a Real Doll. New York: Avon Books, 1995.

Luscombe, Belinda. "Seen and Heard." Time Magazine 150, n12, 22 Sept. 1997: 103.

Magro, Albert M. "Why Barbie is Perceived as Beautiful." Perceptual and Motor Skills 85, n1 Aug. 1997: 363-75.

Mandeville, Glenn A. Barbie Doll Collector's Handbook. Grantsville, MD: Hobby House, 1997.

Manes, Stephen. "For the Barbie Doll's New Clothes." New York Times 24 Dec. 1996: A2+.

Mannix, Margaret. "The Big Barbie Bonanza." U.S. News and World Report 119, n23 11 Dec. 1995: 118-20.

---. "Barbie Madness: Mattel Says It Will Make More 1995 'Happy Holiday' Dolls." U.S. News Jan. 1995: 1-2.

Manos, Susan. The Wonder of Barbie: Dolls and Accessories 1976-1986. Paducah, KY: Collector Books, 1987.

---. The World of Barbie Dolls: An Illustrated Value Guide. Paducah, KY: Collector Books, 1986.

Mason, Tom. "What Makes Barbie a Girl's Favorite Doll?" Investors Business Daily: Executive Update 12 Apr. 1995: 1-2.

Mattel Inc. Original Barbie Doll Theme. [Online] Available http://www.barbie.com, April 5, 1998.

---. "Welcome to Barbie.com: Official Barbie Doll
Web Site." [Online] Available
http://www.barbie.com, Jan. 3, 1998: 1-10.

Maurstad, Tom. "Barbie: Deep Look at Shallow
Subject." Salt Lake Tribune 14 Dec. 1996: 1-3.

McCampbell, Marlene. "Plastic Explosive."
Entertainment Weekly (1997): 79.

McClary, Andrew. Toys With Nine Lives: A Social
History of American Toys. New York: Linnet
Books, 1997.

McDonough, Yona Zeldis. "What Barbie Really Taught
Me." New York Times 25 Jan. 1998: 70.

McKenzie, Jean. "Barbie Gets a Whole New Look."
[Online] Available http://www.barbie.com,
1998: 1.

Melillo, Marcie. The Ultimate Barbie Doll Book. Iola,
WI: Krause, 1996.

Mieszala, Lorraine. Collector's Guide to Barbie Doll
Paper Dolls: Identification and Values. Paducah,
KY: Collector Books, 1997.

Miller, Compton. Who's Really Who. London:
Harden's Books, 1997.

Miller, Wayne G. Toy Wars and the Epic Struggle
Between G.I. Joe, Barbie, and The Companies
That Make Them. New York: Times Books,
1998.

Mitchard, Jacquelyn. "Much Ado About Barbie: You
Can Dis Her, but It's Hard to Dismiss Her."
Parenting 8, n3 Apr. 1994: 87.

Morgenson, Gretchen. "Saturation Barbie?" Forbes Magazine 160, n9, 20 Oct.1997: 46-47.

Morris, Kathleen. "Valley of the Doll." Business Week n.3563, 12 Feb.1998: 46.

Mulrine, Anna. "Barbie Joins the Real World." U.S. News 2 June 1997: 1-2.

Norton, Kevin I., and Steven Dank; Timothy S. Olds; and Scott Olive. "Ken and Barbie at Life Size." Sex Roles: A Journal of Research 34, n3-4 Feb. 1996: 287-95.

"Notes From Outer Space." Canada and the World Backgrounder 60 Jan. 1995: 20-21.

Olds, Patrick. The Barbie Doll Years 1959-1996: A Comprehensive Listing and Value Guide of Dolls and Accessories (2nd Ed.). Paducah, KY: Collector Books, 1997.

Patai, Raphael. Myth and Modern Man. Englewood Cliffs, NJ: Prentice-Hall, 1972.

Phlegar, Phyllis. "When Your Modem Gets the Message 'No One is Home'." People Magazine Oct. 1994: 1-3.

Piercy, Marge. "Barbie Doll." [Online] Available http://www.capecod.net/~tmpiercy/ April 5, 1998: 1.

Pipher, Mary. Reviving Ophelia: Saving the Selves of Adolescent Girls. New York: Putnam Group, 1994.

Pollitt, Katha. "Why Boys Don't Play With Dolls: Children Get the Message Loud and Clear: Can We Change What They Hear?" New York Times Magazine col.3 Oct. 1995: 46.

Pratt, Jane. Beyond Beauty. Indianapolis: Clarkson
    Potter, 1997.
Press, Eyal. "Barbie's Betrayal: The Toy Industries
    Broken Workers." The Nation 263, n22, 30 Dec.
    1996: 10-15.
Priest, Susanna Hornig. Doing Media Research: An
    Introduction. London: Sage, 1996.
Quan, Tracy. "Understanding Barbie-Phobia." [Online]
    Available
    http://desires.com/1.2/words/docs/barbie1.html,
    Sept. 2, 1995: 1-2.
Quigley, Mary W. "Beyond Boy Toy."
    Good Housekeeping Mar. 1998: 73.
Rakow, Lana F. "Rethinking Gender Research in
    Communication." Journal of Communication
    (1986): 11-21.
Rana, Margo. Barbie Doll Exclusively for Timeless
    Creations: Identification and Values: Book 3.
    Grantsville, MD: Hobby House, 1997.
---.   Barbie Exclusives: Identification and Values.
    Paducah, KY: Collector Books, 1996.
---.   Collector's Guide to Barbie Exclusives:
    Identification and Values Featuring: Department
    Store Specials, Porcelain Treasures and Disney.
    Paducah, KY: Collector Books, 1995.
Rand, Erica. Barbie's Queer Accessories (Series Q).
    Durham, NC: Duke UP, 1995.
Randolph, Laura B. "Living Dolls." Ebony 53, n3 Jan.
    1998: 22-23.
Redmond, Melanie C. "You Can Tell It's Mattel."
    Philadelphia Daily News 20 Nov. 1997: 67.

Reuters. "Messing With Success." Philadelphia Daily
    News 18 Nov. 1997: 15.

Reynolds, Jason. "Barbie Does Denali." Outside
    Magazine Feb. 1998: 24.

Riddick, Kristin. "Barbie: The Image of Us All."
    [Online] Available
    http://xroads.virgina.edu/~class/barbie/barb.html,
    Jan. 3, 1998: 1-18.

Robertson, Pamela. "Too Much of a Good Thing: Mae
    West as Cultural Icon." Film Quarterly 51, n1
    Fall 1997: 61-63.

Robins, Cynthia. Barbie: Thirty Years of America's
    Doll. Chicago: Contemporary Books, 1989.

Rosaldo, Michelle Zimbalist. Women, Culture, and
    Society. New York: Stanford UP, 1974.

Rosenberg, Tina. "The New Age Barbie is an Old-
    Fashioned Doll." New York Times 147, s4, col.1,
    30 Nov. 1997: WK8.

Rupp, Rebecca Ann. Doll Treasures (Barbie).
    Grantsville, MD: Hobby House, 1997.

---.   Treasury of Barbie Doll Accessories: 1961-1995.
    Grantsville, MD: Hobby House, 1995.

Sapsted, David. "Barbie, 38, Loses Her Glamorous 80's
    Image." Electronic Telegraph Issue 908 [Online]
    Available
    http://www.telegraph.co.uk/home.html, Nov. 18,
    1997: 1-2.

Sarasohn-Kahn, Jane. Contemporary Barbie: Barbie
    Dolls 1980 and Beyond. Norfolk: Antique Trader
    Books, 1997.

Schneider, Cy. "Origin of Barbie." Children's
Television Script (1987): 1-2.

Schnurnberger, Lynn. "Doll-ing, You Look Fabulous!"
TV Guide 44, n50, 14 Dec.
1996: 10.

Sellers, Patricia. "Women, Sex and Power." Fortune
Magazine 5 Aug. 1996: 1-14.

Settle Robert, and Pamela Alreck. Why They Buy,
American Consumers Inside and Out. New York:
John Wiley and Sons Inc., 1989.

Shapiro, Susan. "My Mentor, Barbie." The New York
Times Magazine col. 1, 6 Nov. 1994: 84.

Shibano, Kelko K. Barbie in Japan. Grantsville, MD:
Hobby House, 1994.

Slate, Barbara. Best of Barbie. New York: Marvel
Books, 1997.

Steele, Valerie. Art, Design, & Barbie: The Evolution of
a Cultural Icon. New York: Exhibitions
International, 1995.

Steiner, Susie. "Barbie Knocks 'Em Dead in the
Greatest Toy Story of Them All."
Associated Newspapers Ltd. 26 Nov. 1997: 1-2.

Stevenson, Nick. Understanding Media Cultures: Social
Theory and Mass Communications. London:
Sage, 1995.

Stipp, David. "Mirror, Mirror, On the Wall, Who's the
Fairest of the Them All?" Fortune Magazine 134,
n5, 9 Sept. 1996: 86-89.

Streicher, Helen White. "The Girls in the Cartoons."
Journal of Communication (1974): 125-29.

Strohmeyer, Sarah. Barbie Unbound: A Parody of the Barbie Obsession. New York: New Victoria, 1997.

Summers, Beth. A Decade of Barbie Dolls and Collectibles 1981-1991. Paducah, KY: Collector Books, 1996.

Thompson, Gary. "Bond and Barbie: Dolled-Down for the 90's." Philadelphia Daily News 19 Dec. 1997: F-6.

"Toy Tech." Time 150, n22, 24 Nov. 1997: 38.

Turner, Maureen. "Maureen Turner Visits a Real Life Dream House." [Online] Available http://sunsite.unc.edu/stayfree/11/barbie.htm, Apr. 10, 1998.

Westenhouser, Kitturah. The Story of Barbie. Paducah, KY: Collector Books, 1994.

Westfall, Ralph, and Harper W. Boyd Jr. Cases in Marketing Management. Burr Ridge, IL: Richard D. Irwin, 1961.

White, Michael. "Mattel Plans Barbie With Less Bosom, More Waist." Charlotte Observer 17 Nov. 1997: 1-2.

Williamson, Judith. Consuming Passions: The Dynamics of Popular Culture. London: Marion Boyars, 1995.

Willis, Susan. A Primer for Daily Life: Studies in Culture and Communication. New York: Routledge, 1991.

Wilson, Craig. "Barbie Traditionalist Skeptical of Change." USA Today 18 Nov. 1997: 1A+.

Wolf, Naomi. <u>The Beauty Myth: How Images of Beauty</u>
<u>Are Used Against Women</u>. New York:
Anchor Books, 1992.

Yoe, Craig. <u>The Art of Barbie.</u> New York: Workman,
1994.

Author Bio

Kristin Noelle Weissman is a graduate of Beaver College and holds a degree in Corporate Communications with a specialization in Marketing and a concentration in Business Management. She is a member of the National Dean's List, and has been nominated for the Margaret LeClair Interdisciplinary Writing Award, American Women's Business Award, Who's Who Among Students in American Universities and Colleges, and Who's Who Among American Young Professionals. Currently, Kristin is living in New Jersey and has a career in marketing management.

LaVergne, TN USA
12 November 2009
163919LV00002B/25/A